HOW TO AVOID ENVIRONMENTAL LITIGATION

The 2nd Edition - **Expanded**

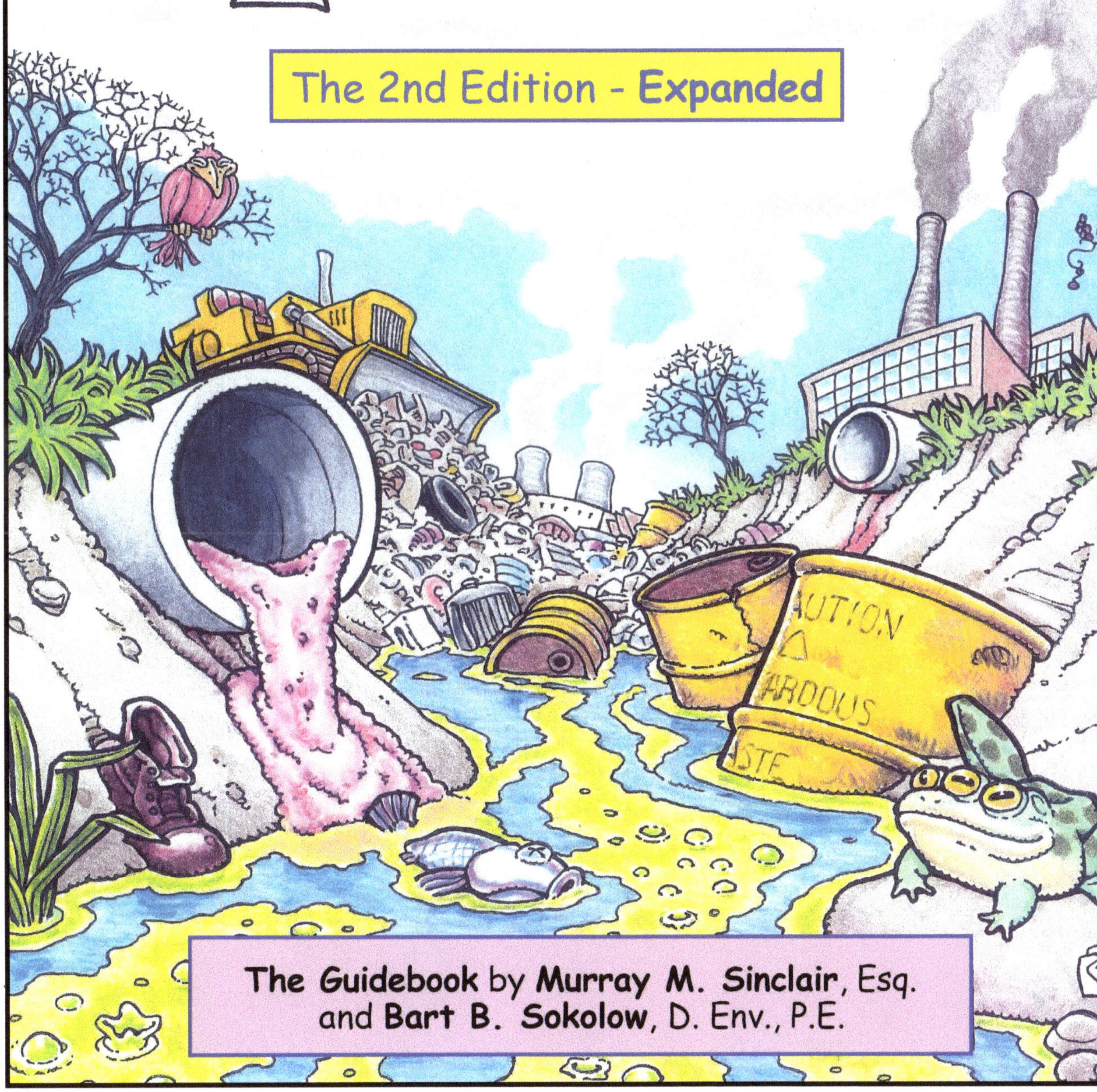

The Guidebook by **Murray M. Sinclair**, Esq.
and **Bart B. Sokolow**, D. Env., P.E.

How to Avoid
Environmental Litigation

Second Edition

by
Murray M. Sinclair, Esq.
Bart B. Sokolow, D. Env., P. E.

Two Guys Publishing

How To Avoid Environmental Litigation: Second Edition.

Published by Two Guys Publishing Company, 5354 Aldea Avenue, Encino, California 91316.

Visit our website at http://www.environmentaldatapages.com for information or more technical information which may be useful in addressing environmental issues.

Second Edition paperback ISBN: 979-8-218-12107-5

Cover illustration & logo by Rick Geary
Other illustrations licensed through Abobe Stock and Shutterstock

ACKNOWLEDGMENTS

The authors are indebted to Zachary Gidding for his tireless efforts and exceeding good cheer in copy editing this book.

In addition, artist Rick Geary's inspired cover illustration compelled us to finish what we started the first time around and to come back to it again and drop our lines to see what else we can reel up from the murky depths of the esoteric environmental swamp mankind has both inherited and created in this strange world we're living in.

Further, the authors want to thank the many clients, colleagues and associates whose experiences helped the authors to apply the principles and approaches presented in this book for others to learn from.

Working on this second edition was much less lonely than the original, as the authors were aided by two esteemed colleagues who are both giants in their field, Robert Ettinger and Jeremy Squire. These gentlemen were kind enough to contribute guest chapters to the text. Robbie Ettinger's chapter on vapor intrusion makes extremely ethereal and vague concepts accessible to the average lunkhead. Jeremy Squire does the same to make remedial technologies understandable to those of us who normally find such things incomprehensible.

ABOUT the AUTHORS

MURRAY M. SINCLAIR

Prior to entering the practice of law, Murray Sinclair was the author of a prizewinning series of mystery novels (*Tough Luck L.A.*, *Only in L.A.*, and *Goodbye L.A.*). These hard-boiled fictional adventures, however, pale in comparison with the bizarre and fascinating cases he has handled as an environmental lawyer over the last 30 years.

Mr. Sinclair represents an array of corporate and individual clients in the environmental arena. After graduating with honors in English from the University of California at Santa Barbara and obtaining his M.F.A. in Professional Writing from the University of Southern California, Mr. Sinclair attended Southwestern University School of Law. He has been an active member of the Los Angeles County Bar Association, serving as Associate Editor of the Environmental Law Section Newsletter in 1993-1994 and as Editor-In-Chief in 1994-1995. Mr. Sinclair was the Chairman of the Environmental Litigation & Insurance Committee of the L.A. County Bar Association Environmental Law Section in 1995-1996 and 2000-2001. He has written and lectured on environmental litigation and environmental coverage issues for both private and public organizations.

Mr. Sinclair is the founder of Murray M. Sinclair & Associates, Attorneys at Law, in Los Angeles, California.

He can be reached at: (310) 826-2700 or email at: murray@murraysinclairlaw.com.

BART B. SOKOLOW

Dr. Bart B. Sokolow, P. E., is founder and president of Environmental Advisors, Inc., an environmental consulting firm that provides highly specialized expertise and a breadth of capabilities in soil, air, water and energy regulatory matters, remediation, compliance and litigation support/ expert testimony across a continuum of environmental issues.

Dr. Sokolow consults with law firms and insurers to assist in the defense and prosecution of responsible parties, the cause(s) and origins of contaminant sources, and estimates of cost-to-cure for large scale environmental claims covering a broad range, from small dry cleaning shops to major shopping centers, manufacturing facilities and Superfund sites across the country. He has served as an expert in interpreting environmental data and regulatory consequences arising from environmental problems, and is able to translate and communicate complex and technical scientific findings for clients and attorneys in accessible terms.

He has served as a consultant to the U.S. Environmental Protection Agency and U.S. Department of Energy on the Resource Conservation and Recovery Act (RCRA), worker health-and-safety issues, and groundwater monitoring technical-enforcement documents.

Dr. Sokolow routinely provides forensic peer review services for real-estate related environmental documentation to banks, insurers, oil-and-gas pipeline companies and real-estate developers. He also has overseen environmental remediation of numerous contaminated properties, including performing engineering reviews of underground storage tank maintenance and removal programs.

He previously served on the Environmental Policy Review Board of the Los Angeles Unified School District to review practices pertaining to mold and fungus health-risk assessments and to establish protocols to comply with state regulatory guidelines for K-12 school sites and methane gas intrusion in existing construction.

A "triple Bruin," Dr. Sokolow earned both his bachelor of science degree in biotechnology and human factors, and his master's degree in energy and kinetics (studying nitric oxide emissions from gas turbines) from UCLA's Samueli School of Engineering, and his doctorate in environmental sciences and engineering also from UCLA. He later was a professor in the UCLA environmental sciences and engineering doctoral program. Dr. Sokolow is a registered professional engineer in the state of California.

He can be reached at 818-907-6565 or drbart@techstuff.com.

TABLE of CONTENTS

Introduction
(Operating Instructions)

If you were our client, we would tell you the only way to avoid environmental litigation would be to never buy property, but instead, live in a cave, assume the fetal position, and never venture out. Despite this admonition, we suspect that there may be times when the possibility of litigation will become an issue. This book will attempt to arm you with all we've got: basic, practical, current, and useful knowledge. The more you know about environmental issues and what you can do about them before they happen to you, the better you will be prepared to avoid a financial crisis. Even after the fact, you can potentially reduce your financial liability. In addition, you may be able to prevent further property damage and environmental exposure to third parties and regulatory authorities if you use the advice that follows. It may be possible to reconstruct a roadmap of what you know environmentally to help chart your future direction. The information in this book may assist you in reducing the costs of future remediation on your site. It may also assist you in dealing with the regulators. You will be able to assess where you fit in relation to third parties—that is, determining who may be liable to you or to whom you may be potentially liable if you take no action.

Environmental problems, for example, may occur on an adjacent property, just next to yours. The fact that the contamination did not obviously occur on your property does not immunize you from potential liability from the source of the problems next door. You might laugh at your penny-pinching relative or friend—you know, the packrat type who saves every shred of paper. Yet there may be a method to their madness. Why? Remember those old insurance policies they had stored in an old shoebox that you thought were worthless? Those old scraps of "worthless" paper may be the modern-day equivalent of a gold nugget. They could provide the means to pay for an environmental cleanup if the policies were written any time before 1987. Hint: check whether your Comprehensive General Liability (CGL) insurance policy contains a pollution exclusion clause, especially one that includes a "sudden and accidental" exception for property damage caused by: (a) an accidental and abrupt spill, (b) overfill, or (c) leak either originating onsite or migrating onto the site from an offsite source. The insurance policies may prove useful for more than fire kindling.

Though most of us would rather stare into the sunset than think about potential litigation, we hope this book brings you just a small sense of relief. The more you understand about events on your property, the more you can relax, knowing your assets are protected.

If a bit of knowledge can be dangerous, this book could be a one megaton detonating device. If you have questions based upon your reading of any chapter or sections of this book, you must seek help from an environmental engineer, an environmental lawyer, or even personnel from a regulatory agency.

Environmental litigation is not a standalone sport. You need competent company. This book is designed to serve as an expanded checklist to avoid environmental litigation. We assume that the reader has received or expects to receive a regulatory notice from local regulatory authorities, or from the state or federal government. We expect the letter will indicate that the reader is presumed to be a potentially responsible party (PRP), that the regulatory authorities have physically or visually inspected or observed the cause for concern, or that they have been informed that a neighbor has concern about activities on your property causing problems on his or her property. As a potential litigant, you need to know enough about a pollution case to be dangerously effective. The initial question is: What actions, if any, can you take to avoid receiving this letter?

Initial Action

The thesis of this book is that environmental disputes don't have to wind up in court. Trials can be won or lost before they ever take place, based on the environmental counsel's ability to promptly and accurately perform an effective initial evaluation of his or her client's liability exposure in the very early stages of the case, even before the action is filed or the time to answer the complaint arises. Before you get to that point, there are many ways to avoid or reduce the costly outlays of time and money.

These suggestions may not avoid litigation. They may, however, narrow your focus, which will result in considerable savings in those most important areas of time, money, and aggravation. Please note, the topics we cover here are generic and we have used California codes and regulations as examples. Every state has its own version and its own laws that will be different but deal with the same substantive issues. If there are no state regulations in a particular area, EPA guidelines may apply, acting in the place of state regulations.

We have designed this book with the idea of providing help for the technically challenged property owner or lessee, business owner or operator, affected neighbor or non-environmental lawyer. We have provided enough technical information to enable these parties to spend their initial time and money developing strategies for prevention rather than on attorneys' fees. We cannot stress strongly enough, however, that the technical information provided in this guide is merely a starting point. To establish a foundation or a necessary database, you'll need legal counsel and a capable environmental consultant to investigate technical and legal issues with greater depth and specificity.

Finally, please note that we have designed the Table of Contents to serve as a "cheat sheet" or road map for the initial critical inquiry.

Chapter I:

What Type of Contamination is at Issue?

The type of contamination of concern can be critical to such issues as legal jurisdiction, as well as whether the cleanup is justified, or even required for public health and safety reasons. For instance, as discussed below, the federal Superfund Law, legally known as the Comprehensive Environmental Response, Compensation and Liability Act of 1980 (CERCLA)[1], is only concerned with the release or threatened release of hazardous substances as defined by the Act. Why do we seemingly state the obvious? Because of political nuances, the Superfund Act does not oversee the cleanup of any oil products. This federal law does not deal with oil at all. In fact, it specifically excludes petroleum oil products. If the contamination at issue relates to oil, it must be cleaned up under RCRA, the federal Resource Conservation and Recovery Act. The United States federal district courts have exclusive original jurisdiction over all CERCLA actions.[2] Therefore, federal court jurisdiction may not be appropriate if

---

1. The Comprehensive Environmental Response, Compensation and Liability Act, 42 U.S.C. § 9601, et seq. was first enacted in 1980, and subsequently amended in 1986 "to provide a solution to the growing number of 'uncontrolled inactive hazardous waste sites' and to remedy the severe environmental problems caused by extensive negligent hazardous waste disposal practices." *Southland Corp. v. Ashland Oil, Inc.*, 696 F.Supp. 994, 998 (D.N.J. 1988) quoting *United States v. Price*, 577 F.Supp. 1103, 1109 (D.N.J. 1983). Approximately 1,300 sites are on the National Priorities List for Superfund cleanup, and it is estimated that 1,700 more sites will eventually be added. Long term cleanups have been completed at only approximately 220 sites based on governmental expenditures of approximately $1.5 billion per year. A Rand study concluded that one-third of all money spent on cleanups has been spent on legal fees. See J. Acton & L. Dixon, Superfund and Transaction Costs (1992).

2. 42 U.S.C. § 9613I.

- hazardous substances are not at issue in the action which has been brought against the alleged potentially responsible party ("PRP") (that's likely you! Cue your attorney); or
- the plaintiff prosecuting the claim against you is mistaken in the assumption that the chemicals used and/or wastes generated by you contain hazardous substances.

If, however, a release or threatened release of a hazardous substance has occurred or is on the verge of occurring, liability under the strict liability provisions of CERCLA is virtually certain.[3] The only remaining issue will be the extent to which you as a current or past owner or operator, or person arranging for disposal of hazardous substances, will be entitled to contribution from other liable parties.

CASE STUDY 1:

Dry-Cleaner Issues

Let's start with something simple: The client owns a dry-cleaning business. He has received a love letter from either

- the California Department of Toxic Substances Control,
- the Regional Water Quality Control Board,
- the local fire department,
- the local health department,
- the next-door neighbor, or
- his landlord.

3. 42 U.S.C. §9601, et seq., imposes liability on all past and present owners or operators of a facility including those who have arranged for disposal or transport of hazardous substances to a facility where a release or threatened release of hazardous substances has occurred which has caused the plaintiff to incur response costs consistent with the National Contingency Plan (NCP) 42 U.S.C .§9607(a).

He tells you he runs a clean operation—a closed-loop system—and always follows the rules. And we're sure he does. Cue the violins. . .

He's fighting a losing battle. It doesn't matter what he does. If PCE or "Perc" is his solvent of choice, like the swallows returning to Capistrano, that solvent will find its way back into the subsurface soil and also possibly into the groundwater, depending on the soil lithology and depth.

The fluids he uses to clean clothes will migrate through his concrete floor if anything spills or leaks onto that floor—and spills and leaks are inevitable from worn gaskets, open dry cleaning machine doors, filling the machine with fresh solvent, and disposing of spent dry cleaning fluid. And please don't assume that we're talking about large quantity leaks or spills. We have seen million-dollar cleanups result from one-gallon spills.

The TCE and PCE did not evaporate. It is now under the concrete—in the soil.

The most likely place to find it is out the back door (or down the backroom sink or toilet) in older dry cleaners where old-time operators used to dump the separator water generated by the older machines.

And oh boy, once that Perc gets into the sewer lines, it will visit the entire neighborhood! It doesn't matter if the lines are completely intact without cracks or fissures. Perc worms its way through the couplings in the line and weeps through the clay material of the line itself.

The issue is the anthropogenic production of greenhouse gases (GHG) like methane, carbon dioxide, and volatile organic chemicals like *perc* (or tetrachloroethene just a different naming architecture) which degrades over time to *TCE* (trichloroethylene or trichloroethene—again a different naming architecture) which over time degrades to vinyl chloride. It is difficult to age-date the use of PCE or TCE because these chemicals do not decay at a quantifiable rate.

Why is this important? Because typically, there have been numerous owners of the dry cleaning business occupying the space. All of them operate differently and evidence different standards of care. They also replace their dry-cleaning equipment over time; typically, the newer the equipment, the less likely there are going to be substantial hazardous releases from it. In addition, at some point in time (around the year 2000 and after) the type of solvent typically used in dry cleaning machines changed from PCE to a petroleum-based solvent less likely to cause environmental damage if released onto the floor, or into soil or groundwater. This is all to say, you will have to figure out the history of the site without age-dating the PCE or TCE, unless the chemical contains certain unique markers, or you can determine when a spill occurred from studying the contaminated soil column and comparing that against the operational history of a site.

A. Hazardous Substances

The term "hazardous substance" is defined in Section 9601, Paragraph 14 of Title 42 of United States Code (i.e., 42 U.S.C. § 9601(14)). Waste which is listed as hazardous under Section 9601 includes any waste that is listed under Section 3001 of the Resource Conservation and Recovery Act (RCRA) or any waste that exhibits the characteristics of hazardous waste identified under 42 U.S.C. § 6921. [4]

---

4. See, *US v. Northernaire Plating Co.*, 670 F.Supp. 742, 746 (W.D. Mich.1987); *US v. Vertac Chemical*, 671

Remember that oil or petroleum products, such as, gasoline, diesel fuel, and waste oil are not considered hazardous substances under CERCLA, even when those products contain hazardous substances (e.g., leaded gasoline).[5] Under what is called the "petroleum exclusion," these hydrocarbon-based products have been excluded from jurisdiction under the federal Superfund Act.[6] There is a pertinent exception: oil sump[7] wastes containing drilling muds, cuttings and other oil production wastes may not be covered by the petroleum exclusion if they are not capable of being refined.[8] A defendant typically has the burden of proving the applicability of the petroleum exclusion.[9] In general, though, unless hazardous substances are at issue, or the requirements of a RCRA claim can be met,[10] federal court jurisdiction may not be proper. As discussed below, most courts take the "one molecule" approach to imposing CERCLA liability, where the presence of any material deemed hazardous is sufficient. If the waste is not identified on the RCRA list (42 U.S.C. § 6921) or specifically listed as a hazardous substance in the Code of Federal Regulations, 40 C.F.R. § 302.4 (the Environmental Protection Agency's designations of CERCLA hazardous substances pursuant to 42 U.S.C. 9602), the waste can still qualify as a hazardous substance if it exhibits *any* of the following characteristics of hazardous waste, as established by the Environmental Protection Agency (EPA) under RCRA: a) ignitability; b) corrosivity; c) reactivity; or d) toxicity.

F.Supp. 595, 613 (E.D. Ark. 1987).

5. *Wilshire Westwood Assoc. v. Atlantic Richfield Corp.*, 881 F.2d 801 (9th Cir. 1989)

6. 42 U.S.C. § 9601(14).

7. A sump is any cavity, hole, compartment, or vault located in the ground.

8. *Cose v. Getty Oil*, 4 F.3d 700 (9th Cir. 1993).

9. *Nixon-Egli Equip. Co. v. John A. Alexander Co.*, 949 F. Supp. 1435, 1443 (C.D. Cal. 1996).

10. In brief, liability may be imposed against any past or current owner or operator of property where solid or hazardous waste has been handled, stored, treated or disposed in such a way that it "may present an imminent and substantial endangerment to health or the environment." Although RCRA operates similarly to CERCLA as a strict liability statute, the relief under RCRA is prospective and injunctive only; the citizen suit provision, unlike that of CERCLA, does not provide a remedy that compensates for past cleanup costs. See, 42 U.S.C. § 6972(a)(1)(B). Further, the Supreme Court has advised that certain limits should be placed on the "imminent and substantial endangerment" aspect of the statute. *Mehrig v. KFC Western, Inc.*, U.S., 116 S.Ct. 1251 (1996). ("An endangerment can only be 'imminent' if it 'threatens to occur immediately.'" [quoting Webster's Dictionary])

These designations are very significant; they are important benchmarks regarding your liability. Ignitability[11] and corrosivity[12] are relatively easy to determine. Reactivity and toxicity, however, are somewhat more complex.

1. Reactivity

Reactive chemical wastes may be those which are unstable and can react violently with water, generating toxic gases or fumes, or possibly exploding. Phosphorous, for example, will explode upon contact with water. Even if the chemical substance in question is non-hazardous, it will be designated as a hazardous substance if it is capable of

- combining with other chemicals and/or substances so as to create a hazardous substance, or
- breaking down or decomposing to a substance or chemical which results in the creation of a hazardous substance.

11. Ignitable waste may be liquid (less than 24% alcohol by volume with a flash point less than 60º Celsius), solid (capable of causing fire by friction, absorption of moisture or spontaneous chemical change), or a compressed gas or oxidizer.

12. Corrosive wastes are characterized by a pH of less than 2 or more than 12.5 or are liquids that corrode steel at a rate 6.35 millimeters per year. A pH of 7 is considered neutral, a pH of 1 is very acidic and a pH of 14 is very "basic" (e.g., sodium chloride).

CASE STUDY 2:
The Fishing Expedition

We call this case study "The Fishing Expedition" in honor of our client who constantly accused the EPA of trying to hook him with liability. In contaminated landfill disposal cases, each person or business entity that has arranged for the disposal of either nonhazardous or hazardous waste at a disposal facility may be a PRP with respect to resulting contamination. In these situations, it is typically argued that waste disposed at the landfill will break down or decompose under landfill conditions to release hazardous substances, even if the original waste is not hazardous. For example, in one such case, it was alleged that a client had disposed of a chemical, 1,3 butadiene (a gas component released as an unintended byproduct in the manufacture of synthetic latex) at a landfill Superfund site.

Using existing EPA research documentation, the authors of this book were able to demonstrate that because the "half-life"[13] of the 1,3 butadiene in the waste deposited at the landfill was no greater than four hours, it was inconceivable that any measurable quantity of this chemical contributed to the groundwater contamination problem at the site. It was also helpful that there were no existing chemical analyses revealing evidence of the actual presence of any 1,3 butadiene in the groundwater at the site.

13. The term "half-life" has been over time been defined two ways. It is the time required for a quantity to reduce to half of its initial value. Originally its meaning was strictly scientific, describing radioactive substances, specifically identifying the amount of time after which half of a particular radioactive substance would have decayed into another substance. "Half-life" has since become a commonly used colloquialism to identify the time period in which half of any compound or chemical has either dissolved, evaporated, or decayed into some other chemical. For example, the medical sciences refer to the biological half-life of drugs and other chemicals in the human body.

2. Toxicity

Toxicity is determined by analyzing leachate[14] from the samples of the waste at issue and comparing each contaminant's concentration levels in samples of the contaminated soil or groundwater to the appropriate regulatory limits set by local, state, or federal agencies. In 1990, the EPA developed a test called the Toxicity Characteristic Leaching Procedure (TCLP) to determine the leaching potential of waste under landfill conditions. If a waste can pass the TCLP test, and it is not otherwise classified as hazardous, it should not be deemed hazardous. The TCLP's previous incarnation was the Extraction Procedure (EP) test, which you may see referenced in older technical documentation on the subject. There are seventeen specific chemicals for which the TCLP has been developed. These tests are neither cheap nor instantaneous. Basically, if a leachate is shown to migrate, or move, through a medium (soil or water) based upon the results of the TCLP test, you may have a problem. A positive TCLP test could indicate that your leachate may have, or could in the future, contribute to groundwater contamination at a landfill site.

The following factors would have a bearing on whether there is a probability of contamination by leaching:

- Vertical distance from your waste to groundwater
- Depth from the surface
- Whether any subsurface geologic barriers exist which would preclude liquid transport.

Each site, we have learned through experience, is truly unique.

"Capable of Generating a Hazardous Substance" versus "One Molecule"

Most courts take the restrictive "one molecule" approach to CERCLA liability. Under this theory, you as a PRP may incur liability where your waste contains any amount of a hazardous substance, even minuscule traces, or just one "molecule." Under this theory, dumping a box of Kellogg's Raisin Bran would make the dumper a PRP, since breakfast cereals contain trace amounts of heavy metals, like copper, zinc, and iron.

---

14. "Leachate" is the liquid that is produced when groundwater percolates through soluble waste materials as it moves through underground soil and rock. The term "leachate" or "leaching" also applies to liquid chemical wastes migrating through underground soil and rock, with or without the aid of groundwater.

This is exactly what the US Federal Ninth Circuit Court of Appeals has ruled on the subject. Although trace levels of hazardous substances are present just about everywhere, the Court of Appeals has agreed with EPA's interpretation of the Superfund law, i.e., that CERCLA's definition of "hazardous substance" has *no minimum level requirement.* As such, the court (Kozinski, J.) observed that "read as the EPA suggests, CERCLA seems to give the agency carte blanche to hold liable anyone who disposes of just about anything. Drop an old nickel that actually contains nickel? A CERCLA violation. Throw out an old lemon? It's full of citric acid, another hazardous substance."[15]

Some courts take a more practical approach. For instance, in a federal lawsuit, *US v. New Castle County* (D. Del. 1991) 769 F.Supp. 591, 597, the PRP disposed of polyvinyl chloride (PVC) resin in a landfill. Bear in mind that the white pipes used nationwide for lawn water irrigation systems are made of PVC. While vinyl chloride is a known carcinogen and hazardous substance under CERCLA, polyvinyl chloride (essentially very long chains of vinyl chlorides) is not reactive and does not exhibit similar impacts on human health (i.e., does not cause cancer via dermal exposure or inhalation). Although the PVC in question did contain trace amounts of unreacted vinyl chloride, the parties agreed that the resin did not "depolymerize, decompose or degrade to form vinyl chloride under normal landfill conditions."[16] Therefore, because it could not be shown that the resin would generate or release a hazardous substance at the site, the district court granted summary judgment for the defendant on the vinyl chloride issue, freeing the defendant from any liability. The court said that where "a defendant's waste is a non-hazardous substance, a plaintiff must show that the defendant's waste is *capable* of generating or releasing a hazardous substance at the site in order to show that the defendant's waste contains a hazardous substance within the meaning of CERCLA."[17] The popular white PVC piping, for example, is safe enough to be used in many municipal water systems and lawn irrigation systems.

It would not seem logical for CERCLA liability to be imposed in every situation where hazardous substances are present in microscopic amounts that do not appear to present a threat to public health or the environment. Other courts, however, have rejected the New Castle approach "to the extent that it requires a plaintiff to demonstrate that a defendant's waste is capable of generating or releasing a hazardous substance at the actual

---

15. *A & W Smelter and Refiners, Inc. v. Clinton* (9th Cir.1998) 146 F.3d 1107, 1110.

16. Id. at 597.

17. Id.

site."[18] Given how strictly some courts construe CERCLA, alternative legal defenses to liability need to be considered, such as "did the alleged release of a purported hazardous substance from your waste cause the response costs as required under CERCLA?" We discuss these defenses further in Chapter 7.

B. Petroleum Products

Petroleum hydrocarbon fuel in the subsurface environment is distributed among the following major phases:

- Fuel vapors as a component of soil gas
- Fuel adsorbed (i.e., attached) to soil particles
- Liquid fuel in open pore spaces of soil particles
- Liquid fuel floating on the groundwater table (the "oily sheen")
- Fuel dissolved in groundwater

1. Three Generic Petroleum Products

There are three generic petroleum products that show up in soil and ground water pollution cases: gasoline; diesel; and waste oil.

a. Gasoline

Gasoline consists of petroleum hydrocarbon substances in the carbon chain ranging from C4 to C12 (that is, molecules consisting of four to twelve chained carbon atoms). The fewer carbon atoms, the more volatile the hydrocarbon will be. Gasoline has a unique smell. The reason? It's caused by the volatility of the constituent chemicals in the gasoline. The most abundant chemical components are benzene, toluene, ethylbenzene, and xylene.

---

18. *State of Arizona v. Motorola, Inc.*, 774 F.Supp. 566, 574 (D. Ariz. 1991) See also *B.F. Goodrich v. Betkoski*, 99 F.3d 505, 517 (2nd Cir. 1996) (Although plaintiff must show a release or threatened release, "the additional releasability requirement of product breakdown finds no support in CERCLA.")

Thus, the acronym BTEX is routinely used to describe laboratory tests to identify all four of the components. Before the 1990s, in California, gasoline contained lead additives. This is significant in hydrocarbon fingerprinting and age-dating of petroleum hydrocarbon fuel contamination. The presence of lead strongly indicates the fuel was in use before a certain point in history. Effective January 1, 1996, leaded gasoline was banned by the Clean Air Act for use in new vehicles other than aircraft, racing cars, farm equipment, and marine engines.

Benzene is the key contaminant in gasoline because of its public health implications. It is a known carcinogen which causes leukemia. Benzene is also flammable and prone to explosion in locations where it has accumulated over time. A specific EPA laboratory test procedure, EPA 8015,[19] is used to identify gasoline contamination in soil by measuring levels of BTEX. To identify gasoline in water, the EPA test 8020 is used.

b. Diesel Fuel

Diesel fuel is different from gasoline and consists predominantly of hydrocarbon molecules in the range of C12 through C20. As a result, diesel fuel is less volatile than gasoline. Critically, diesel fuel does not contain benzene. This is important because the presence of benzene becomes another way to determine the source of soil and groundwater contamination on your property. Assume that an underground tank holding gasoline is the purported source of soil contamination on your site. If the laboratory tests show no benzene in the samples, the contamination could not have been caused by leaks from that tank. In addition to its use as vehicle fuel, diesel has also been used historically as a solvent in the automobile maintenance and construction industries. Diesel fuel is toxic and flammable. Since diesel is a longer-chained hydrocarbon than gasoline, it is thicker and denser. It is also easier to identify and clean up because 1) it moves more slowly through soil and groundwater, and 2) it evaporates more slowly in air (it stays around as a liquid longer). These characteristics give diesel a longer residency time. Environmentally speaking, it *perseveres*.

c. Waste Oil

Waste oil is relatively easy and inexpensive to remove or clean up. Waste oil typically consists of used oil drained from automobile engines, crankcases, or transmissions, or from routine

19. See www.epa.gov/epahome/index/ for a "Guide to EPA Test Methods" that indexes all EPA approved soil tests methodologies and references to other relevant data.

maintenance operations of manufacturing machinery. Its constituents are hydrocarbons that range predominantly from C18 and higher. One of this oil's characteristics is its high thickness or viscosity (its flow characteristics are typically slow like molasses), making it easy to trap or isolate in a collection system. Typically, waste oil will not migrate quickly through soil. Additionally, waste oil is generally insoluble, and its density is substantially greater than water. Even if waste oil is found in groundwater, it will likely not mix with or dissolve in the groundwater.

2. Test Methods

A combination of standard EPA test methods, in addition to elaborate geochemical methods for characterization of petroleum products, can be applied to define characteristics of environmental samples. There are many sites where the source of hydrocarbon contamination is not visually obvious. For these sites, forensic environmental chemistry techniques can help to determine the contamination source (if present) and its history. Additional environmental problems result when soils become saturated with released fuel. In these situations, the hydrocarbon fuel components can migrate through the soil, both vertically (penetrating groundwater) and laterally. Once groundwater is contaminated, it has the potential to enlarge the contaminated area, exacerbating any environmental problem and potential cleanup.

One test that can be used is a *screen test* for soil such as the EPA 418.1 test. "Screen tests" have nothing to do with Hollywood starlets. It means that a chemical test is used to determine whether there are any hydrocarbons present in the sample. It will not tell you which compounds there are, nor in what quantities.

The EPA 418.1 test identifies total recoverable petroleum hydrocarbons (TRPH)—that is, those hydrocarbon molecules with one carbon to those molecules with 46 carbons, which includes such common hydrocarbon compounds as asphalt, heavy waste oils, and even tars. As such, the EPA 418.1 test can be used to identify diesel or other hydrocarbon contamination. But extreme caution must be used in implementing this test. It does not yield any quantification of concentration, quantity, or volume—just the *existence* of TRPH. The EPA 8015D test—a modification of the 8015 test for gasoline—can be used to detect diesel fuel components and to identify diesel contamination. The EPA 418.1 test, on the other hand, is a screening test to determine the presence of any petroleum hydrocarbons, rather than the presence of a specific compound. It is a binary test, determining whether a sample has petroleum hydrocarbons or not.

It is not uncommon for inadequately trained or unscrupulous consultants to misuse the EPA 418.1 test to obtain extremely high readings of total recoverable petroleum hydrocarbons (TRPH). The results may then be alleged to show high levels of gasoline or diesel contamination. However, the EPA 418.1 test is not that definitive. What the test may actually be detecting is the TRPH level resulting from the existence of particles of tar or common asphalt. These non-migrating, harmless, rock-hard petroleum hydrocarbons were commonly used as fill material for the construction of real-estate projects in the 1960s and 1970s. In California, for example, the State Department of Transportation (CALTRANS) sold the broken-up remnants of old highways and roads to real-estate developers to be used as fill for new construction. Asphalt can also be detected by the EPA 418.1 test at sites where a parking lot or driveway material has been incompletely removed from a site's ground surface before construction began. These EPA detection tests can detect quantities of hydrocarbons in the parts per billion range, and so TRPH resulting from asphalt is sometimes detected in locations where subsurface samples were obtained by piercing an existing asphalt driveway or road, if the drill bit was not cleaned before testing or interacting with the soil. Neither asphalt nor tar pose a significant threat of migration or movement through the soil. Further, if a consultant's testing protocols are not rigorous, they can accidentally test the presence of the asphalt that they had bored through to test the underlying soil, if the location is in a paved parking lot.

Caution should be exercised if the EPA 418.1 test is the sole laboratory analysis used. Be careful if a contractor suggests additional investigation, substantial soil excavation, additional soil and groundwater sampling, or remediation expenditures based solely upon the results from a 418.1 test. You must obtain additional validating data with other more specific testing methods before proceeding.

To summarize, the EPA 418.1 test is typically used as a field "screen test" to test for waste oil contamination, in conjunction with appropriate substance-specific tests, such as the EPA 8020 test to find BTEX (gasoline) components in water, or the EPA 8015 test modified to test for diesel fuel components in soil. Be careful if the only test used to justify further expenditures of your money is the EPA 418.1 test. You need to obtain additional chemical analytical data to confirm the detection of specific hydrocarbons. A chemist specializing in petroleum hydrocarbon chemistry will likely be needed.

CASE STUDY 3: Digging for Fool's Gold

A hospital had removed several gasoline underground storage tanks ("USTs") that were no longer being used. These tanks had been installed for the use by staff doctors as a luxurious convenience but were now simply cumbersome historical artifacts and costly to keep in the ground. Current permitting standards required costly upgrades to double-walled containment and ancillary water detection systems outside the tanks.

In the process of investigating the site, the hospital's environmental consultant tested the soil in a large perimeter around the location of the USTs. They found petroleum hydrocarbon contamination that they told the hospital administrator needed to be cleaned up.

The hospital's consultant then proceeded with an expensive cleanup using an advanced technology that used bugs to eat the hydrocarbons, rather than simply physically removing the soil. The hospital's advisors thought this approach was more cost effective.

Two issues arose. First, the site had previously been a dumping ground for the California Department of Transportation (CALTRANS). As highways and streets were rehabbed, built, or modernized, CALTRANS dumped the remnants of previous asphalt road materials on the site. The result was that there were small particles and larger pieces of asphalt, used pavement oils, and so on, strewn throughout the site and mixed in with the soils. While there was long-chain petroleum hydrocarbon contamination in the soil, *it was also inert and not going anywhere–the bits of asphalt were not mobile and not a threat to groundwater.*

But—besides the fact that the cleanup was marginally if not completely unnecessary, an even bigger surprise came when the consultant declared that the cleanup had been a successful application of their bugs—and submitted their final bill for *$8 million*. What is the problem, you might ask? Well, it was a lot of money, but if that's what it took to clean up the property, you might say well, okay. That wasn't what really made us mad. It was the testing approach that the consulting firm had used to test the soil before they began. They used an ASTM 418.1 test, which tests for carbon chain hydrocarbons ranging from gasoline to hard immovable asphalt, *without distinction*. The contamination levels of petroleum hydrocarbons in the soil that *actually* needed to be cleaned up were never determined.

Since we knew CALTRANS had used the site as a dumping ground for many years, there was an excellent chance that what the environmental firm had identified without further examination were pieces of solid asphalt, which weren't going anywhere. Worse, how do we know that the cleanup they had performed had actually cleaned up anything? There was no evidence of what the starting levels of petroleum contamination were. There was no data.

The case was settled for a fraction of the asking price, and the hospital sued its errant consultant for the remainder.

3. Hydrocarbon Fingerprinting of Soil Contaminants

The origin and historic timing of a chemical release into the environment can be difficult to determine. Most petroleum hydrocarbon contamination results from spilling, leaking, explosion, dumping, or regular use of hydrocarbons. The forms of hydrocarbons you are most likely to encounter are fuels, like the gasoline used in cars and diesel fuels used in machinery and large trucks. Other common petroleum hydrocarbons are lubricating oils, used in everything from wristwatches to automobiles. All these products have been "refined." They have been filtered and chemically modified from crude oil that was pumped out of the ground.

Crude oil is initially transported by rail, truck, or pipeline to an oil refinery, where it is chemically separated into its various valuable secondary products. This refining process produces fuel oil for furnaces, gasoline, asphalt for paving, diesel fuel, jet fuel, kerosene, naphtha, and fine lubricating oils. These refined products are distinguished from one another by molecular weight and the length of the carbon chains (measured by C4–C40; the higher the number, the heavier the oil that constitutes the basic backbone of the product) and the type of additives that have been integrated into the product. Gasoline, for example, tends to contain anti-knock agents, lead scavengers, and antioxidants.

Product formulations have also changed over time. For instance, leaded gasoline was first marketed in 1923,[20] and until 1960 tetraethyl lead (TEL) was used as the only anti-knock agent. Over time, state and national air quality laws phased out and eventually eliminated lead additives. Prior to 1975, diesel fuel was primarily straight-chained, while post-1975 diesel fuel was thermally cracked. This distinction can be determined analytically with a small volume of product, thereby providing a time frame for when the product was available.[21]

Other less environmentally harmful compounds, such as ethers and alcohols, have been blended in with gasolines to maintain high octane ratings and reduce vehicle emissions of carbon monoxide. Methyl tertiary-butyl ether (MTBE) has been blended with gasoline since approximately 1979. Its first documented use was in 1980 on the East Coast and 1990 in California. MTBE caused public concern because (along with other gasoline components) it can contaminate groundwater when underground fuel tanks leak. MTBE moves faster in water than other fuel components and, in small amounts, renders drinking water unusable. On March 25, 1999, Governor Gray Davis declared that MTBE presents an environmental risk to California and directed state agencies to take steps towards eliminating its use in California gasoline by December 31, 2002. The Governor found that

---

20. L.M. Gibbs, "Gasoline Additives—When and Why," in SAE Technical Paper Series (International Fuels and Lubricants Meeting and Exposition, Tulsa, OK, Oct. 22-25, 1990); Bois, Thomas J., II and Luther Bernard J., Groundwater and Soil Contamination, § 8.4, Refined Products Characterization (John Wiley & Sons, 1996).

21. http://206.117.189.123/bmorrep.htm, "Forensic Techniques for Establishing the Origin and Timing of a Contaminant Release," Robert D. Morrison, Ph.D., DPRA Inc., 100 E. San Marcos Blvd., Suite 308, San Marcos, California 92069

it was possible to eliminate use of MTBE on January 1, 2003, without significantly risking disruption of the availability of gasoline in California.

Why Are We Telling You About All These Strange Chemicals?

Simple. These chemicals can be used to "age date" evidence of hydrocarbon use. For example, if an oil spill found in California contains tetraethyl lead (TEL) it would be possible to determine that the contaminating hydrocarbon release occurred before 1992 (since TEL has been banned in in California since 1992). Other local use bans may vary, but leaded gasoline was banned altogether for use in new vehicles effective January 1, 1996. Thus, if you bought a contaminated property after 1992, you could show that liability should not attach, under most legal theories of liability. If MTBE is present in the resulting hydrocarbon analysis, we know the dates of its first documented use on each coast, and so we can age-date the release.[22] If you sold the property before 1990, MTBE in the sampling results would be an indication that the soil contamination probably occurred after you sold the property. It could not have occurred "on your watch."

Through analysis, you can also tell where in the world, and especially in which oil fields, crude oils were produced, and perhaps how long its refined products have been in the ground. Chemical data exists based upon the degradation of crude oil. Every crude oil production field has unique "chemical markers," or fingerprints based upon its geologic age, location, and subsurface geology. These characteristics are unique for each oil field and can be used by experts to tell where fuel oils were discovered and subsequently refined.

22. I. Kaplan et al., 1995, "Pattern of Chemical Changes in Fugitive Hydrocarbon Fuels in the Environment." Society of Petroleum Engineers, SPE 29754, SPE/EPA Exploration & Production Environmental Conference, Houston TX (March 27-29, 1995).

4. Hydrocarbon Age-Dating Techniques

a. Aerial Photography Interpretation

The successful use of this technique depends upon the dates of your involvement as the owner, lessee, or operator of the property in question. After the dates of ownership or use have been determined, aerial photographs for the same dates can usually be purchased from either private vendors or university collections—or, in many cases, initially reviewed for free on Google Earth. You can then retain an expert in aerial photographic interpretation.

Where Do You Get Aerial Photos?

Follow That Car!

One free location is on Google Earth. It's available on any computer connected to the internet. It's free. Just type in the address. The site has aerial views and, in most locations, street views. The icon appears in the top row of any photo. It displays a clock with an arrow apparently "moving" counterclockwise, i.e., backward in time. If you click on it, you will be able to observe a timeline of available historic aerial photos of the location on the screen. By clicking the arrows shown, you can observe aerial photos of the site on the dates within the date range that are displayed. If there were substantial changes to the site, or a spill, it may be visibly noticeable from the earlier aerial photos that you can now examine.

Why are aerial photos important? If, for instance, earlier aerial photographs show evidence of black smoke belching from the manufacturing facility on your property ten years before you took title, this fact could be used as evidence to expose or shift liability from you to the prior owner or operator of the property.

The photos would be useful to you for other reasons as well. They may provide keys to locate the "hot spots" where hazardous operations or dumping may have occurred on the site. Potentially, only a portion of the property may be contaminated. You may be able to identify specific parts of the property that could be isolated for future cleanup. If specific, discrete areas of concern can be identified, future cleanup or remediation costs may be reduced.

Under such a scenario, the prior owner might be encouraged to clean up selected sections of the property. You may then be able to enjoy the use of the property without disruption, or at least minimal interference—and reduced cost.

b. Chemical Fingerprinting

Sophisticated analytical techniques can identify more than just the age of hydrocarbons in soil. Chemists can now examine fuel composition in the soil as a function of when the formulation was used and by whom, based upon the identification of additives associated within specific companies or product brands, during discrete historic time periods.

Specific additives will display characteristic patterns in, for example, a readout of a gas chromatograph sample. These "chemical fingerprints" may allow experts to identify whether a particular oil sample was produced by a particular oil refiner. The fingerprint may allow a determination of a time period, based upon when the additive was produced or used. If the chemical(s) of concern (a term of art used by regulators to identify regulated or restricted chemicals) is known, the date of its first known commercial availability can identify the earliest date that it could have been present on your site. For instance, as discussed above, MTBE first came on the scene in 1980 on the East Coast and 1990 in California.

c. Association of the Chemical with a Manufacturing Process

If you can determine how the site was used historically or, specifically, what chemicals or what product(s) or device(s) were manufactured there, experts such as chemical process engineers, industrial engineers, or chemists in the specific field of manufacture can help identify probable locations on site for incidents, accidents, or spills. For example, in the manufacture of printed circuit boards, the "wet area" of a facility historically would become a likely source for spillage of TCA (tetrachloroethane). Since early manufacturing techniques were not geared to recycling of used process fluids; the liquid solvents were allowed to spill onto the floor—and into—the soil through cracks or gaps in the concrete or other flooring material—that is assuming the ground was even covered. Historically, such areas were not always covered with concrete but were open to the ground within the manufacturing facility. If you know the property used to be a circuit board factory and can determine where the former "wet area" was, you may have an idea of where and what sort of contamination you may expect to find.

d. Chemical Degradation Modeling

Chemical degradation models are used to estimate the length of time a hydrocarbon or chlorinated solvent has been in the ground. This technique can be helpful in determining who is to blame for a particular contamination, or for developing allocation models in cost recovery cases. You can obtain a "chain of title" for a real-estate parcel through a request to a title company or county recorder, which is a review of the previous ownership of the parcel. Suppose you have reviewed historic aerial photographs and have determined that earlier uses were not just grazing land or corn fields, but manufacturing. Perhaps, through the title research, you may find there were several prior owners on your site who were likely not farmers. At this point, a degradation analysis might determine either when the contamination was initiated (when the "accident" occurred), or when the maintenance problems on specific equipment began.

Please realize that some of the techniques we've mentioned are interrelated. Chemical degradation can help identify a time period, and chemical fingerprinting can further refine it. It is like a chess game with some of the pieces missing. It is always important to recognize that this is not an exact science. It is a hunt for the truth. Sometimes the truth is revealed under a rock that turns out to be an asphalt chunk of an old roadway from some other area of the city. Sometimes it appears in the soils directly beneath a dry-cleaning machine, or in a musty jar of oil at the back of an old storage shed on the property.

e. Reverse Groundwater Modeling

These analytical techniques together, or in combination with existing data, can lead to identification of the timing and origin of a contaminant release. This technique is a lot like the Lewis and Clark expedition to the Northwest. Or the final scene from the movie, *The Bridge on the River Kwai*. As the river unexpectedly recedes, Alec Guinness's character finds the detonation wire to blow up the bridge in the river bottom. He proceeds to slowly expose the wire as the train approaches the bridge.

The technique of reverse groundwater modeling uses some of that guile. An expert can look at what you have, working backward to figure out how it got there. What you can calculate historically in terms of determining when a hazardous release occurred (and how long it has continued) depends upon the data you must work with and what you are looking for. Imagine you are dealing with the site of a former dry cleaner. It can be complex to calculate the travel rate through soil of a molecule of PCE (tetrachloroethylene, perchloroethylene, or "perc"—a common dry cleaning fluid) or TCE (trichloroethylene—a chemical breakdown product of PCE and a common metal solvent or cleaner) or from the contamination source (e.g., a metal plating tank or dry cleaning machine) to the groundwater beneath your property. How complex depends upon the chemical (specifically its molecular weight and density), the geology, soil type, the groundwater gradient and flow direction and numerous other factors, including the analysis of other contamination source areas that may be combining with, or intermingling with, the contamination on your site. You would also need to determine the time it took for the TCE- or PCE-laden water to migrate down through the soil column to the water table to determine how long and through what type of geology the water traveled. Then, you would need to determine the types of geology and soil conditions through which the groundwater travels. Obviously, this is a complex process which, though highly scientific and expert-driven, can be subjective and, at times, somewhat speculative.

f. BTEX Analysis

By convention, the volatile petroleum hydrocarbons Benzene, Toluene, Ethylbenzene, Xylene (BTEX) are combined in one group of analyses, because of their potential toxicity. The concentration of these compounds can be measured by EPA test Methods 8015B and 8021B (for soil); or a combination of 8260B and either 8021B or 8015B (for contamination in groundwater) using different sample introduction techniques.

BTEX measurements are mandated by the EPA to determine if there is a potential human health risk, based upon their measurements of exposure. The mere presence of BTEX isn't the issue. The significant point is whether the analysis indicates that there is a pathway for human contact, either by ingestion or inhalation or dermal (skin) contact.

If there is no existing pathway for human consumption or exposure, there is no threat to public health and welfare.

According to the EPA,[23] for there to be a risk, all components of an exposure pathway must be complete, as follows:

- Source
- Transport mechanism
- Exposure point
- Receptor
- Exposure route

By regulatory definition, for there to be a human health risk, there must be a pathway for the contamination to be exposed to a subject. If there is no pathway, there is no risk, and therefore, no need for remediation.

CASE STUDY 4:
The Mystery of the Indoor Air Issue

Our client was trying to lease his 30,000 square foot warehouse to a major HMO which intended to transform the large building into office space. The HMO had hired its own engineering firm to perform an indoor air quality test. This test, called an TO-15, uses several Summa canisters[24] that are empty but are calibrated to fill with air over an 8-hour period. The engineering firm came out and did the test.

The lab results showed that the T0-15 test had failed. Yet the building was vacant and had been unoccupied and

23. U.S. EPA 1989. *Risk Assessment Guidance for Superfund, Volume II: Environmental Evaluation Manual.* EPA/540-1-89/001.

24. Summa is a brand of air canister for collecting air samples, and is about the size of a propane tank such as one might attach to a gas barbecue grill.

closed for a relatively long period of time (and unfurnished, only the wood studs were showing every 16 inches). We soon learned that while the building was empty, the owner had been storing paint cans in the building, *and* workers had been tracking in soil from the newly seeded lawn outside the warehouse. We advised the client that those paint cans and the fertilizer from the newly seeded landscaping could be causing the failed T0-15 test.

So, what did we do next? Simple: we opened all the doors, rented some gigantic fans, placed them in all the doorways, and left them on for 2 weeks. The prospective tenant's engineering firm retested. The tests failed again. The client was getting nervous, the HMO wanted out of the pricy deal. The situation was grim. We then called OEHHA (the Office of Environmental Health Hazard Assessment at the California Department of Toxic Substances Control [DTSC]). We discussed our predicament with DTSC staff toxicologists about the failed T0-15 tests. The toxicologists asked what we had been testing. "The building," we attempted to explain. "No," they responded, "you need to test *worker exposure.*" The HMO's engineering firm had been testing the building itself, rather than the pertinent human health risk issue.

What we needed was to rent a portable HVAC system for the 30,000-square-foot building for two weeks, and then re-test the indoor air for worker exposure. It passed after we ran the portable HVAC system for a few weeks to approximate normal working conditions. It wasn't "cheating" to have a HVAC system operating during the T0-15 test–rather, we needed to create normal working conditions to accurately test the indoor air for worker exposure. We succeeded in creating normal working conditions by creating a regulated temperature-controlled environment like you would have in a normal office building.

The relative concentrations of specific volatile aromatic hydrocarbons (another name for BTEX-like chemicals that you can smell—and that are bad for your health) in environmental samples is key to determining the length of time that gasoline has been present in an aqueous environment.

C. Is There Mold Contamination?

We can't do better than to refer you to "Basic Facts about Mold and Dampness," a brief article on the CDC website (www.cdc.gov/mold/faqs.htm). It's also worth looking at the EPA website on mold (www.epa.gov/mold). Both turn down the volume on this volatile issue and present the basic facts.

Mold contamination is very common in buildings and homes. While most mold is harmless, it is ubiquitous. Mold will grow in places with excessive moisture, such as around leaks in roofs, windows, or pipes, or where there has been flooding. Mold grows well on paper products, cardboard, ceiling tiles, and wood products. Mold can also grow in dust, paints, wallpaper, insulation, drywall, carpet, fabric, and upholstery.

The most common indoor molds are *Cladosporium Penicillium*, and *Aspergillus*. Less common but of concern is *Stachybotrys chartarum*, the "black mold" that people seem to be most concerned about because it has garnered much media coverage. *Stachybotrys chartarum* is a greenish-black mold. It can grow on material with a high cellulose content, such as fiberboard, gypsum board, and paper. It can grow where there is residual moisture resulting from water damage, water leaks, condensation, water infiltration, or flooding. Constant moisture is required for its growth.

1. How do molds get in the indoor environment, and how do they grow?

Mold is found both indoors and outdoors. Mold can enter your home through open doorways, windows, vents, heating and air conditioning systems, and older planter boxes affixed to the outside of homes. Mold in the air can also attach itself to clothing, shoes, and pets, and can be carried indoors by air flow. Many building materials provide suitable nutrients for mold to grow. Wet cellulose materials, including paper and paper products, cardboard, ceiling tiles, wood, and wood products, are particularly conducive for the growth of some molds.

2. How do you know if you have a mold problem?

Large mold infestations can usually be seen or smelled. As US Supreme Court Justice Potter Stewart wrote in his opinion on pornography (*Jacobellis v. Ohio* (1964) 378 US 184), "I know it when I see it."

3. How does mold affect people?

Exposure to damp and moldy environments may cause a variety of health effects—or none. Some people are sensitive to exposure to mold. For these people, exposure to mold can lead to symptoms such as stuffy nose, wheezing, and red or itchy eyes or skin. People with allergies to mold or with asthma may have more intense reactions. Severe reactions may occur among workers exposed to large concentrations of mold in occupational settings—for instance, farmers working around smelly, moldy hay. Severe reactions may include fever and shortness of breath.

In 2004, the Institute of Medicine (IOM) found there was sufficient evidence to link indoor exposure to mold with upper respiratory tract symptoms, coughing, and wheezing in otherwise healthy people; with asthma symptoms in people with asthma; and with hypersensitivity pneumonitis in individuals susceptible to that immune-mediated condition. Other recent studies have suggested a potential link of early mold exposure to development of asthma in some children, particularly among children who may be genetically susceptible to asthma development. It has also been suggested that selected interventions that improve housing conditions can reduce morbidity from asthma and respiratory allergies.

A link between other adverse health effects—such as acute idiopathic pulmonary hemorrhage among infants, memory loss, or lethargy—and molds found inside homes (including *Stachybotrys chartarum*), has not been proven. Further studies are needed to find out what causes acute idiopathic hemorrhage and other adverse health effects. There is no specific blood test for mold. Some physicians can do allergy testing for possible allergies to mold, but no clinically proven tests can pinpoint when or where a particular mold exposure took place.

Mold exists everywhere—in the air and on many surfaces. Certain molds are toxigenic, meaning they can produce toxins (specifically "mycotoxins"). Hazards presented by molds that may produce mycotoxins should be considered the same as other common molds which can grow in your house. Not all fungi produce mycotoxins and even those that do will not do so under all surface or environmental conditions. Mold growth, which often looks like spots, can be many different colors, and can smell musty. Color is not an indication of how dangerous a mold may be. Any mold should be removed and the moisture source that helped it grow should be removed.

4. Who is most at risk for health problems associated with exposure to mold?

People with allergies may be more sensitive to molds. People with immune suppression ailments or underlying lung disease are more susceptible to fungal infections. Individuals with chronic respiratory disease (e.g., chronic obstructive pulmonary disorder, asthma) may experience difficulty breathing. Individuals with immune suppression are at increased risk for infection from molds.

5. How do you keep mold out of buildings and homes?

It is always appropriate to perform routine maintenance inspection of buildings for evidence of water damage and visible mold and to correct conditions causing mold growth (e.g., water leaks, condensation, infiltration, or flooding) to prevent that growth.

6. What is a simple test for mold exposure—what should trigger further examination?

You get a call from a client. He owns an apartment house, she owns an office building, or they own a large retail complex. Tenants are complaining of scratchy and hoarse throats, sneezing, and odd smells.

What should you do? You should ask them to leave. Why? If the building environment is causing their ill health, it should disappear or at least significantly abate after they leave the building. If their symptoms don't moderate, then the building is not the cause of the problem. They should seek medical care. It's not your problem.

7. How to Confirm Your Need to Perform Mold Cleanup and Remediation

Initially, you need to confirm that there is actually mold to clean up. This will require a CIH (Certified Industrial Hygienist—see below) to perform contemporaneous testing of both the premises and a neutral location. The neutral site test is to confirm that any mold you find is exceptional and not typical of the area where your building is located. Testing data from a "mold" environment in Billings, Montana, for example, will be distinctly different from test data derived deep in the Amazon rain forest.

This warning comes from experience. Both authors were involved with an $8 million site cleanup. At its conclusion, the engineering firm confirmed the site was clean. The problem was they never had performed the same onsite testing protocols before they began their work. There was no data that identified the site had the contamination they purported to have cleaned up before they began their remediation. In other words, there was a significant question whether the site was *ever* initially contaminated.

8. Now, mold has been reported to be present at a property I lease or own. How do I test the mold?

If you can see or smell mold, a health risk may be present. You do not need to know the type of mold growing in your home, apartment building or commercial structure. No matter what type of mold is present, you cannot ignore it. It should be removed.

Emphatically, mold investigation and remediation companies are rife with unqualified, huckster consultants and contractors. The industry is highly unregulated. In addition, there are some MDs, allergists, and neuropsychologists who have developed highly questionable (and very profitable) theories regarding the dangers of exposure to mold. You must vet them with extreme care because they can do great (emotional) harm by alarming people for no reason. They can also destroy property for no reason as they purportedly eradicate the mold at issue. And most of all, they can wipe you out financially.

We know of no state organization pertaining to licensing mold contractors. However, the American Board of Industrial Hygiene (ABIH) offers a certification process whereby a qualified individual may become a Certified Industrial Hygienist (CIH). Since 1960, the ABIH has been the world's largest organization for certifying professionals in the practice of industrial hygiene. The ABIH website states that a CIH is an individual who has met the minimum requirements for education and experience, and through examination, has demonstrated a minimum level of knowledge and skills in the following areas:

- Air sampling and instrumentation
- Analytical chemistry
- Basic science
- Biohazards
- Biostatistics and epidemiology
- Community exposure
- Engineering controls / ventilation
- Ergonomics
- Health risk analysis and hazard communication
- IH program management
- Noise
- Non-engineering controls
- Radiation—ionizing and non-ionizing
- Thermal stressors
- Toxicology
- Work environments and industrial processes

Qualified toxicologists also offer expertise in this area.

When a mold investigation is performed, it should be done through or with the oversight of a CIH. Similarly, when a remediation contractor performs work on a commercial or residential structure, it should be directed by a CIH. There is no way around this. Furthermore, the written protocol that a CIH can prepare establishes a protocol for remediation that is legally binding. It has the weight of law in California. It will hold up in court.

9. Liability Issues

Associated with the health issue is the liability issue you will confront if you are a property owner. If the mold problem is allowed to fester, it will not only spread but it will stigmatize the property like a Scarlet Letter, depressing the desirability of the property and thus its value.

Under California law, and under state law in most jurisdictions in the United States, all leased residential premises are subject to the implied warranty of habitability, which imposes on the landlord the obligation to maintain leased dwellings in a habitable condition throughout the term of the lease.[25] The standard here is strict liability for injuries to tenants caused by defects in the premises.[26]

In short, the premises must be clean, sanitary, free from all accumulations of debris and filth, and fit for residential occupation.[27] A concentration of indoor mold sufficient to affect the health of the tenant makes the building unfit for occupancy, and thereby breaches the implied the warranty of habitability, simultaneously constructively evicting the tenant from the premises and breaching the lease agreement between the landlord and tenant. Tort damages (including punitive damages) and breach of contract damages are available to plaintiffs. Pursuant to the attorneys' fees provision in the lease agreement between the parties, fees will often be available to plaintiffs as the prevailing party in the civil action which may be filed by the tenant. The failure of a landlord to comply with applicable statutes and ordinances may also constitute negligence per se.[28]

Regarding liability under a nuisance theory, most "modern California cases have recognized that, 'The statutory definition of nuisance appears to be broad enough to encompass almost every conceivable type of interference with the enjoyment or use of land or property.'"[29] In short, "the term 'nuisance' is applied to a multiplicity of wrongful acts that may arise out of numerous types of tortious conduct, whether negligent, intentional . . ."[30]

As stated in Section 731 of the Code of Civil Procedure, any person whose property

---

25. *Peterson v. Superior Court* (1995) 10 Cal.4th 1185 (*Peterson*), 1204; *Green v. Superior Court* (1974) 10 Cal.3d 616, 619.

26. *Peterson*, supra, 10 Cal.4th at 1204.

27. Cal. Civ. Code § 1941.

28. *Peterson*, supra, 10 Cal.4th at 1204, fn. 10; Cal. Evid. Code § 669 [failure of person to exercise due care presumed where person violates statute, ordinance, or regulation of public entity].

29. *Mangini v. Aerojet-General Corp.* (1991) 230 Cal.App.3d 1125, 1136, quoting *Stoiber v. Honeychuck* (1980) 101 Cal.App.3d 903, 919.

30. 11 California Forms of Pleading and Practice, Nuisance, §4.1 (Matthew Bender 1992).

is injuriously affected or whose personal enjoyment is lessened by a nuisance may bring a claim for the interference with such interests. As a lessee in possession during the time that the nuisance continued unabated, plaintiff tenants would qualify as persons "whose property is injuriously affected or whose personal enjoyment is lessened" pursuant to § 731. There is no requirement that the complaining party currently be in possession of the affected property.

Damages recoverable for nuisance are governed by Civil Code § 3333 which entitles the injured party to recover an amount to compensate the injured party for all detriment proximately caused by the nuisance. Exemplary or punitive damages may also be awarded in connection with a nuisance claim.

Chapter II:

Where Is the Contamination Located?

The physical location of the detected contamination is critical in the assessment process. While contamination can occur in either air, water, or soil, we will concentrate on water and soil. Why? Releases in air are often immediate, and usually involve compliance problems related to the ongoing daily business operations for specific regulated industries. Soil and groundwater, however, are the main generators of site cleanup costs. They are the time bombs that can increase the scope of a cleanup severalfold. When these time bombs explode, they invariably impact indoor air in commercial and residential buildings, creating serious air problems (as discussed below). Latent property damage may go undetected for decades and may only be discovered later as the result of due diligence investigations related to real estate transactions, property development, or illness or disease in the community. Remember Erin Brockovich?

A. Is the Contamination in the Soil Only?

If the contamination is limited to the soil, thank your lucky stars. Groundwater remediation tends to be a long and costly process. Where groundwater is neither impacted nor potentially threatened, remedial activities are typically more limited. The quantity of contaminated soil can be defined or quantified, and if soil is to be removed, the area can usually be reduced to those specific areas that must be treated or excavated to be brought back to acceptable, regulatory levels.

If no underground storage tanks are involved, the supervision of any soil remediation will typically remain with local agencies such as the fire department or local public works agency. Ordinarily, the state will become involved only if there is a perceived threat to groundwater, since in most states, groundwater is considered public property held in public trust and falls under state administration. Without a threat to groundwater, local regulations typically rule. Check with a local contact in a city government engineering, public works, or the public health department. You can make a "what if" call to find out who to speak to without incriminating yourself. There is usually an assigned duty officer whose job it is to answer phone calls without the need to disclose your name.

1. Types of Soils

Groundwater is found in subsurface bodies called aquifers. An aquifer is an underground river that winds its way through the different types of soil. Depending on the type of soil, the contamination may migrate downward or spread horizontally (laterally) over a larger area and a greater volume of soil, potentially posing a risk to groundwater. The type of soil that has been contaminated dictates how the contamination can be contained or remediated. There are four basic types of soil: gravel, sand, silt, and clay. These soil types are all associated with particular "historic" features of the landscape; that is, they occur in places where streams, lakes, or other landscape features once lay in the geologic past. Each type of soil has different properties when interacting with groundwater and contaminants, and so we'll discuss each in detail.

a. Gravel

Gravel consists of rocky bits or particles (like pebbles). It typically occurs in stream beds that either currently exist or existed in a geological period in the past. It is the easiest conduit for water to move through because there is available air space—called "pore spaces"—between gravel particles. The flow rate of subsurface groundwater tends to be fastest through gravel. Thus, if liquid contaminants are introduced into a gravel environment, they will flow quickly through it to subsurface groundwater and become more pervasive. That is, they will tend to spread out more quickly through the loose soil and become more expensive to clean up.

b. Sand

Sand consists of fine particles and, like gravel, is typically found where streams historically flowed. A pure sand environment is like a gravel environment in that it is quite porous, although sand is more densely packed than gravel. Though the pore spaces are smaller than those found in gravel, this type of soil still allows liquid movement through the soil, albeit at a slower rate. Liquid contaminants may still permeate relatively rapidly through sand, as compared with other types of soil.

c. Silts

Silts are typically found in lakebeds, bogs, and deep ocean areas. Silts are essentially densely packed sands, with even smaller pore spaces. Liquids like water can be "held" within the silts, but still travel through, albeit very slowly.

d. Clays

Clays typically occur in historic lake beds, deep ocean sediments, bays, lagoons, and bogs associated with coastal environments. Clays are difficult to remediate because they are so impermeable. Contaminants tend to adhere to the clay, even beyond the point when the fluids have moved on through the soil to lower depths. Contaminants will adsorb onto clay particles, coating the particles in the contaminant. Adsorption makes various remedial procedures difficult to implement. Clay isn't all bad news, however. Clay soils can form impenetrable "caps" in the soil environment, protecting lower soil and groundwater layers from further contact with liquid contamination from sources or accidents closer to the surface. If contamination reaches a clay layer in the soil environment, the contamination typically will not pass below that "cap," (so long as the cap is intact), remaining confined to areas above the clay layer. A clay "cap" is also called an aquitard or aquiclude. It's like the bottom of a pool or the top of a tent; water is not supposed to penetrate through it in either direction.

2. Is Soil Cleanup Necessary?

If soil contamination is present, you should address the following questions to determine whether a soil cleanup is necessary.

a. Is There a Threat to Groundwater?

The soil contamination plume (the mass of contamination in the soil extending outward from the surface source) should be examined to determine whether it is: a.) static and immobile; or b.) migrating off site, either laterally or downward toward groundwater. The mobility of the plume is critical to evaluating whether you, or potentially others, may be liable to pay for or contribute to cleanup or remediation costs.

Whether groundwater is threatened is relevant not only to the scope of remediation, but to possible defenses to a nuisance or trespass suit over the contamination. The law makes a distinction between a *continuing* nuisance or trespass (where some ongoing activity is causing continuous harm) and a *permanent* nuisance or trespass (where the activity caused harm at a specific point in time).[31] Contamination that is completely static and immobile (such as a release of asphalt, tar, or waste oil), where there is no threat to groundwater, would almost certainly be categorized as a permanent nuisance or trespass. This is an important classification, because the statute of limitations on permanent nuisances and trespasses typically begins to run at the time the contamination occurred, and if the lawsuit was filed too long afterward, you may be able to prevail on a statute of limitations defense if you are sued. In California, the statute of limitations for permanent nuisance and permanent trespass is three years.[32] If the nuisance in question is permanent,

---

31. See *Capogeannis v. Superior Court* (1993) 12 Cal.App.4th 668, 675-676 ["If a nuisance is *permanent,* then in the ordinary case the plaintiff must 'bring one action for all past, present, and future damage within three years after the permanent nuisance is erected. ... Damages are not dependent upon any subsequent use of the property but are complete when the nuisance comes into existence.' If, on the other hand, the nuisance is *continuing,* then '[e]very repetition of [the] continuing nuisance is a separate wrong,' subject to a new and separate limitation period, 'for which the person injured may bring successive actions for damages until the nuisance is abated, even though an action based on the original wrong may be barred,' but '[r]ecovery is limited ... to actual injury suffered [within the three years] prior to commencement of each action' and '[p]rospective damages are unavailable.'" (internal quotation marks and citations omitted)]; see also *Baker v. Burbank-Glendale-Pasadena Airport Authority* (1985) 39 Cal.3d 862, 868-869.

32. Code Civ. Proc. § 338(b).

and the person suing you knew or should have known[33] of the problem three or more years before suing you, the suit would likely be barred.

Continuing nuisances and trespasses are a different beast. The salient feature of a continuing nuisance or trespass is that its impact "may vary over time"—that is, the contamination may continue to spread or worsen.[34] Contamination "may be shown to be a continuing nuisance by evidence that the contaminants continue to migrate through land and groundwater causing new and additional damage on a continuous basis."[35]

The basic legal test for determining whether a nuisance or trespass is permanent or continuing is the "abatability" test. As succinctly stated by the California Supreme Court, "abatable" means that the nuisance can be remedied "at a reasonable cost by reasonable means."[36] It is the plaintiff's burden to present "evidence that the injury is capable of being abated and that the cost of abatement is reasonable."[37] Where a nuisance or trespass is abatable, it is considered to be a continuing one, and the plaintiff can maintain a lawsuit even if the contamination first began outside the statute of limitations.

Even where contamination is alleged to be unlawful or exceeding government standards, such contamination does not automatically establish the nuisance to be continuing rather than permanent, especially where the plaintiff does not seek abatement (i.e., an injunction to stop the contaminating activity) but only monetary damages for the damage.

We will discuss these defenses in more detail in Chapter 7. However, to prevail on a statute of limitations defense on a permanent, tort-based claim such as nuisance,

---

33. The "knew or should have known" concept is also known as the "discovery rule." The point in time that contamination should have been known is a complex concept which has been interpreted by a number of cases over recent decades. See *Mangini v. Aerojet-General Corp.* (1991) 230 Cal.App.3d 1125, 1150 in which if "a person becomes aware of facts which would make a reasonably prudent person suspicious, he or she has a duty to investigate further and is charged with knowledge of matters which would have been revealed by such investigation."; see also *Wilshire Westwood v. Atlantic Richfield Co.* (1993) 20 Cal.App.4th 732, 740 (in which a consultant failed to advise that gasoline odors were present on property, negligence and strict liability claims were barred by statute of limitations because plaintiff is charged with presumptive knowledge so as to commence the running of the statute where plaintiff has the opportunity to obtain knowledge from sources open to his investigation."); *Mortkowitz v. Texaco, Inc.* (N.D.Cal. 1994) 842 F.Supp. 1232 (knowledge that property had been gas station for a number of years "should have put Plaintiffs on inquiry about possible soil contamination.").

34. *Beck v. Southern Pacific Transportation Co.* (1996) 44 Cal.App.4th 1160, 1218.

35. Ibid.

36. *Mangini v. Aerojet-General Corp.* (1996) 12 Cal.4th 1087, 1103 (*Mangini II*).

37. Id. at 1104.

trespass, strict liability, or negligence, you need only show that the plaintiff knew or should have known of the contamination so long ago that the statutory period has lapsed. Three additional things must be proven to prevail on a statute of limitations defense for continuing tort claims such as nuisance or trespass:

- That the nature of the contamination is static and unvarying, not continuing
- That the plaintiff failed to abate the nuisance at a reasonable cost
- That the means employed by plaintiff to remediate the nuisance were unreasonable.[38]

Where the cost of remediation far exceeds the actual harm that would have been suffered by the plaintiff if the property wasn't remediated, you may be able to show that the cost to be incurred is unreasonably burdensome. In addition, in determining whether the methods employed to remediate the property were reasonable, if the plaintiff has not followed appropriate steps in performing site remediation activities, you may be able to show that the means used to abate the contamination were per se unreasonable.

These concepts are cautionary tales or warnings if you're trying to get your own property cleaned up. You must be mindful of cost. Cost effectiveness is an important criterion, not just for your own pocketbook but also for federal and state approvals of cleanup plans. You must also follow appropriate state and federal environmental guidelines in conducting your site investigation and cleanup activities. Make sure the environmental consultant or remediation contractor you choose is in good standing with the regulatory agencies that have jurisdiction over your property—it does you no good to hire a contractor who has been blacklisted. Ask them whether they have ever previously worked with the agencies with whom you're dealing. Then call the agencies and ask about the company's reputation before you hire them. Also, determine whether you have a reporting obligation (in the case of a threat of groundwater contamination, you almost certainly do). If so, you should demand that your consultant obtain regulatory pre-approval for all proposed work before commencing any cleanup activities on your property. Otherwise, it will be difficult, if not impossible, to obtain site closure and secure the ever-coveted "No Further Action" or "NFA" letter you seek, and you may be forced to do the same thing twice to please the regulator.

If a threat to groundwater exists because of soil contamination at your property and you have been aware of the problem for some time but have been slow to pursue those

---

38. Id.

who caused the problem, you may still be able to avoid the statute of limitations bar. Remember: just as you may be sued over the contamination on your property, you can sue as well, but the responsible party may be able to assert the same statute of limitations defense against you. You can assert continuing nuisance and continuing trespass claims against the responsible party, which will include specific allegations that the parties' activities caused the contamination and that the contamination continues to migrate through the subsurface environment, causing harm by threatening to pollute or polluting the groundwater. You might then be able to recover damages for the statutory period prior to the filing of the complaint, and possibly also for damages occurring during the pendency of the lawsuit. The court may also issue injunctive relief, consisting of orders to stop polluting (a prohibitory injunction) or to clean up pollution (a mandatory injunction). These may be imposed in a preliminary form during the case or, in final form, at the case's end.

b. What Are the Applicable Soil Screening Levels?

Numerous sources prescribe limitations on environmental chemical exposure and allowable levels in the environment. You must consult state and federal laws and regulatory guidelines to determine if

- the contamination which is present at your site currently exceeds regulated maximum contaminant levels (MCLs), thereby requiring cleanup;
- the proper investigation has been performed;
- there has been a sign-off or a "no further action" determination from a regulatory agency;
- there exists confirmation for a soil or groundwater problem on the site;
- the cleanup has already been performed, whether the allowable MCLs were exceeded prior to the cleanup; and
- you are acquiring a site which was previously closed with contaminant levels exceeding the current MCLs.

Data from prior soil and groundwater investigations and prior remediation activities can be invaluable. By knowing the benchmark level of contamination, you can determine how much, if any, of the contamination has come from your stewardship of the site.

c. What Type of Soil Is Beneath the Property?

As we discussed above, the type of soil can be an early warning sign of potential groundwater involvement. Gravelly or sandy soil is much more of an easy transport conduit for liquid contamination than clay soil, and so gravelly soil on your site should raise a red flag. Have a geological report prepared before you purchase a property. If the seller is willing to pay for the report, make sure you have input into choosing the consultant who will perform the study and draft the report. If not, it may be worthwhile to pay for the report yourself so you will be able to choose the consultant and control the process. That way, you will be armed with the knowledge of potential problems should a spill or accident occur.

d. What Soil Contaminants Are Present?

Obviously, you must find out what contaminants are polluting the soil, if any. You must understand how to read chemical laboratory reports on soil sampling, as they can be misleading. Imagine a case of suspected gasoline contamination. There may be a chemical lab report finding giving a reading of total recoverable petroleum hydrocarbons (TRPH)—there is oil (or some other hydrocarbon) in the soil. Yet, there may also be a notation of non-detect, or "ND" (meaning no detection of the chemical above the limits of detection reported by the laboratory) of aromatic hydrocarbons, such as the gasoline constituents benzene, toluene, ethylbenzene, and xylenes. These gasoline constituents (BTEX) are known carcinogens that pose a public health risk. Where there is a level of TRPH in the soil but no BTEX, cleanup may not be required (see Case Study 3, above, concerning the TRPH reading which turned out to be immobile asphalt). You may be confronting a hidden, potentially large cost. This could be an issue of testing protocols; that is, whether the proper tests were used to detect the contaminants at issue. Further investigation could find laboratory errors or incomplete testing protocols. Concerned regulators may pursue the investigation based upon this incomplete data. Yet there are still alternatives to dealing with such problems. Use of a health risk assessment to determine pathways of exposure could prove useful.

e. Does the Groundwater Underneath the Soil Contamination Have a Beneficial Use?

Typically, most subsurface water or groundwater is considered drinking water. In California, groundwater would be designated drinking water unless specifically excluded. The California State Water Resources Control Board's (SWRCB) Resolution 88-63 has specific criteria for designating groundwater as non-drinking-water. One of California's regional water quality boards may also make a site-specific non-drinking water determination. SWRCB Resolution 88-63 specifically states that water is non-drinking water quality or "nonbeneficial" if it contains total dissolved solids of over 3,000 milligrams per liter or deliverability of less than 200 gallons per day. Cleanup standards will be less stringent for site soil that is above groundwater designated as non-drinking-water quality (i.e., non-beneficial) than for drinking-water-quality groundwater (i.e., for beneficial use).

f. If the Groundwater Site Is Designated a Beneficial Use, What Is the Vertical Distance Between the Soil Contamination and the Beneficial Use Groundwater at the Site?

Even if the groundwater below the soil is of beneficial use, soil cleanup requirements are dependent upon both the type of soil and the estimated volume of the contaminant plume in the soil. It is possible that a limited site cleanup or no cleanup will be required if

- the soil contaminant plume is small and can be defined;
- the soil matrix is dense (not porous like gravel); and
- the contaminant is a long-chained hydrocarbon (such as waste oil) that will not evaporate easily to become an air quality problem.

For example, the California SWRCB's Leaking Underground Storage Tank Manual (known, believe it or not, as the "LUST" Manual) sets specific cleanup levels that are dependent on several factors, including

- the depth to groundwater from the surface,
- the horizontal distance to beneficial water sources, and
- the contaminant concentration, among other factors.

CASE STUDY 5:

Where's Waldo?

What follows is sort of an obvious question. You should be able to see it, but it's so simple and plain you overlook it. It usually doesn't work, but when it does, it's a total Get Out of Jail Free card. It's a box that needs to be checked, because sometimes if *you* don't ask or explore this issue, no one will. And even if you're wrong, if you're close enough to the border of an area designated as non-beneficial, it makes a big difference to the regulator.

Each area in California has a basin plan that designates water quality. For example, there is a Water Quality Control Plan for the Los Angeles region. However, there are certain exceptions to this plan, and from time to time the regional board passes resolutions, approved in turn by the parent State Water Resources Control Board (SWRCB). On November 2, 1998, pursuant to Board Resolution No. 98-18 adopted by the Los Angeles Regional Water Quality Control Board, the regulatory provisions of the Water Quality Control Plan for the Los Angeles region were modified by removing the beneficial use designation from two specifically defined areas of one ground water basin: the portion of West Basin underlying the Chevron facility in El Segundo and the aquifers underlying Terminal Island and portions of Los Angeles and Long Beach Harbors.

"So what?" you might say. However, this fact was extremely important to a client of ours who owned a VOC-contaminated property a block away from the exempted area. Technically, the client's site was designated beneficial use–meaning the water was potentially useable for drinking or irrigation. However, it was close enough to the non-beneficial use area to inspire the regulator to relax its normally rigorous standards and allow for site closure and the issuance of a No Further Action letter, even though the VOC levels were above the maximum contaminant level (MCL) allowed by federal and state law.

Another part of the equation concerns the total dissolved solids (TDS) count in the site groundwater (see subsection e above, "What Are the Applicable Screening Levels?"). Why would the TDS even matter? What's the reasoning? The TDS in drinking water comes from natural water sources, sewage, urban runoff, industrial wastewater and chemicals used in the water treatment process, and the hardware or piping used to distribute water. Higher TDS can also be present as the result of natural environment features like salt deposits, mineral springs, seawater intrusion, and carbonate deposits. So, simply put, water with a high TDS count is both unhealthy and typically does not taste good. Yuck.

In our situation, we had a double whammy. The site itself bordered the exempted non-beneficial area–plus our TDS lab results showed that TDS was over the 3,000 milligrams per liter limit. Bingo. The regulator stopped harassing the client and issued the coveted NFA letter.

g. What Are the Future Land Uses in the Area?

If the general land use trend in the area is moving toward commercial or industrial development, with diminishing agricultural or residential use, stringent soil cleanup standards may not be warranted. Specifically, if a contaminated soil area is going to be "capped" or covered with asphalt for use as a parking lot, regulators should be reminded of this fact at every available opportunity. In such a situation, natural attenuation (i.e., "no further action") may eventually be more appropriate than performing a costly soil excavation, removal, and disposal. There cannot be a defined health risk if there is no pathway for human health exposure. Covering an area with an asphalt parking lot will effectively prevent airborne pathogens or human health exposure by inhalation or dermal exposure to most chemicals which lie beneath the asphalt.

h. What Are the Potential Health Effects Associated with the Contaminants?

Since the amount of total petroleum hydrocarbons (TPH) does not per se measure the risk or toxicity of the contaminants, the Los Angeles Regional Water Quality Control Board has in the past set screening levels based upon the carbon range numbers of the TPH. The more volatile, lighter-end hydrocarbons found in gasoline (C4-C12) are more mobile, and thus more capable of moving through the soil to groundwater. Heavier-end (that is, longer chain) hydrocarbons—such as those found in lubricating oils and waste oil (C23)—are less capable of movement through the soil. Therefore, the LA Regional Board has higher, more relaxed screening level requirements for the heavier-end hydrocarbons than for the lighter-end hydrocarbons. The lighter-end hydrocarbons travel more easily through the soil. BTEX, the primary constituents of gasoline, are lighter-end hydrocarbons and more volatile, and so are subject to much more restrictive screening levels and/or cleanup requirement levels. In fact, BTEX contaminated soil must be cleaned to MCLs (maximum contaminant levels) primarily because of their high volatility.[39]

39 The MCLs (maximum contaminant levels) for BTEX in soil in California are: benzene = .001 ppm (parts per million); toluene = 0.1 ppm; ethylbenzene = 0.68 ppm; and xylene = 1.75 ppm.

B. Is Groundwater Impacted or Threatened?

1. The Basic Concept and Meaning of Groundwater

The term "groundwater" refers to any underground source of water. Approximately 40% of all beneficial use water in California comes from groundwater. During drought years, when surface water supplies are reduced, California, particularly Southern California, becomes even more dependent on groundwater supplies. The state's groundwater reserves hold about 850 million acre-feet (an acre foot is one acre of water one foot deep and equals 325,900 gallons of water) in nearly 400 groundwater basins beneath about half the land area of California. However, only about 250 million acre-feet can be reached and used.

Groundwater is stored in the spaces between rocks and soil materials in water-bearing formations known as aquifers. Aquifers can extend for hundreds of miles and can be hundreds of feet thick, storing immense amounts of water. The bottom of an aquifer is marked by the impervious barriers (called "aquitards") which water encounters when it moves through the soil. Eventually, water will reach a layer of bedrock or another impervious formation or geologic unit such as clay. Clay is made of particles which are so close together that no water can pass between them. Water collects above this layer and completely saturates the subsurface material where it meets the aquitard. The top of this soaked layer is called the "water table."

Just above the water table, moving into the unsaturated zone, is capillary water, or water that moves upward from the water table by capillary action. The space just above the water table is called the "vadose zone" or "capillary fringe," which characteristically is not completely saturated with water. Between the land surface and the water table is an area called the unsaturated zone (just above the vadose zone), where some water is suspended in the interstices between soil, gravel, or rock particles.

2. Hydrological Cycle

Water finds its way underground through several different transport mechanisms or pathways. Generally, when water evaporates from the land surface and sea, it returns to earth as precipitation (rain, sleet, or snow). The water may then flow into an underground aquifer by percolating downward through gravel and sand in a stream bed. Again, infiltration into a groundwater aquifer occurs much more easily through gravelly and sandy soil than through clay soil. Water may seep onto the ground through crop irrigation, rain, lakes, stream beds, runoff from mountains and hills, or snowmelt in the spring. All these transport mechanisms permit surface water to infiltrate the soils and eventually become groundwater.

Groundwater may be extremely slow moving. While surface water flow is measured in feet per second, it is not uncommon to measure the velocity of groundwater in feet per year. Once a contaminant enters an aquifer, it may take years for the underground basin to replenish itself or for the contaminant to be detected at a monitored well downstream. This slow speed is one critical reason why groundwater contamination poses such serious potential problems. Years or decades may pass before the contamination levels are measured in groundwater sampling wells at distances of as little as 50 to 100 feet from a leak, spill, or accident.

3. Jurisdiction Over Groundwater Contamination

When groundwater contamination problems arise, the California State Water Resources Control Board (the "State Board"), together with its nine regional water quality control boards across the state, operate collectively to protect water quality within the state of California.[40] In addition to possessing the authority to protect the beneficial uses of groundwater in California, the state and regional boards have the authority to protect surface waters such as lakes, creeks, streams, coastal waters, rivers, etc. "Beneficial uses" include not only drinking water, but also uses such as fishing and recreation. The state and regional boards operate under the authority of California's Porter-Cologne Water Quality Control Act, which assigns overall responsibility for water quality protection to the state board and directs the regional boards to establish and enforce water quality standards within their respective boundaries.

The regional boards within the state of California are responsible for protecting the beneficial uses of surface and groundwaters within their respective areas. Each regional board is governed by nine members, all of whom are appointed by the governor and confirmed by the state senate. Each board operates somewhat autonomously. They all

40. Cal. Water Code § 13001.

are required to adhere to the same environmental rules and regulations. They just do it in slightly different ways. The protocols for complying with specific regulations may vary from one region to an another.

Whenever groundwater contamination is an issue in a pollution case, the attorneys and consultants working for you must know and be conversant with the engineering standards and protocols applied by the specific regional board that will have jurisdiction over the property. Each regional board has guidelines or a guidebook which addresses the demands and requirements that it has for protecting water quality in its area.

Boots on the Ground

Don't depend entirely on your lawyer and consultant to read the guidebook and follow it. Get a copy yourself and read it cover to cover. You'll be able to understand more than you think. What you don't understand you can ask your lawyers and consultants to explain. Then through every step of the investigation and cleanup process you'll have some idea of where the project should be going, and you'll be better equipped to keep the project on track if it's in danger of getting derailed.

In addition to being conversant with the applicable regional board's guidebook, your attorneys and consultants must contact the regional board to confirm that the guidebook being reviewed has not been recently revised or altogether replaced by a more current guidebook. This sounds obvious, but it cannot be stressed enough, given that environmental laws and regulations are in a constant state of flux, and the agencies implementing those laws and regulations obviously follow suit. Remember, *there is no "legacy exception" to environmental regulations.* If the rules change tomorrow, you must know what they are and comply with them.

Check the state's website at www.ca.gov, or others, such as

- www.blymyer.com/links/water.html#pcs;
- the California Environmental Resources Evaluation System, at ceres.ca.gov/;
- Leaking Underground Storage Tanks Information System (LUSTIS) at www.swrcb.ca.gov/~rwqcb9/Unit_Home_PageSite_Mitigation Cleanup/UST/LUSTIS/lustis.html; for a list of common acronyms, see our glossary of environmental terms.

Experience has shown that neither your attorney nor your consultant should depend on the other to know what rules and regulations are being implemented or followed by the relevant regional board. Just like how checks and balances are a critical feature of government, it is appropriate for your attorney and environmental consultant to constantly check each other to be certain that they have properly determined which agency would have jurisdiction over the cleanup and, equally important, what regional board requirements apply to the cleanup in question. This is clearly an area where science and law intersect.

For instance, it is not unusual to find oneself in a lawsuit where the plaintiff's consultants have prepared thousands of pages of remedial investigation reports indicating a dire situation. Although superficially convincing due to the sheer volume of paper, the reports may be based on erroneous assumptions of what agency has jurisdiction over the cleanup, and what standards would apply. While the actual standards are sometimes less rigorous than assumed, typically, the error is in favor of "overkill," assuming *more* stringent standards than actually occur. It may be to a consultant's benefit to assume more stringent standards, as it may mean more work for the consultant. In these "overkill" situations, one often finds that: 1.) there has been no communication between the consultants and the regional board; 2.) there has been no examination of remedial alternatives; and 3.) ultimately, the criteria applied by the consultant have little or no relationship to what the regional board requires.

The Regional Board's "mandate" may have been misread simply because no one bothered to contact Board officials to confirm or clarify Board procedures, requirements, or guidelines. While Board literature is replete with guidelines and examples, the chances that your situation will completely follow or perfectly mesh with such "cookbook" examples is remote. Where the data or characteristics of the contamination diverge from guidebook examples or guidelines, it is to everyone's benefit to request clarification from the Regional Board. Otherwise, both time and money may be wasted.

Remember, the Regional Board will not act to perform economic oversight. If your consultants are doing "too much," the Board will not stop them. In other words, regulations recommend but do not require a cost-effective approach to cleanup. The Regional Board's main concern is the protection of the state's waters, not the bank accounts of distraught clients. If more work was performed at greater cost and time than was necessary, the Regional Board will not intervene if the engineering activities followed the Board's basic guidelines and fell within an acceptable standard of care.

Because environmental litigation is somewhat akin to the Wild West, we have had the unfortunate experience of encountering more than a few environmental consultants who have either performed fraudulent remedial investigations and cleanups or who have exacerbated environmental problems and cleanup costs by their active negligence.

For instance, in the fraud category, we have been retained by clients in after-the-fact situations where cleanup costs were between $1 million and $5 million over budget. The consultant assumed a cleanup was necessary without contacting the lead agency having jurisdiction over the site. They performed cleanup work that was not required and had no relationship to the minor environmental problems connected with the site. In these cases, the contamination could have been left in place because it neither threatened the environment (i.e., there was no threat of contamination to groundwater, and the groundwater itself was completely brackish and non-beneficial in use) nor posed any sort of health risk. Minor contamination existed less than one foot below ground surface. It could have been removed by a few workers with a pick and shovel in a few hours or less at a cost of a few thousand dollars. Instead, the dishonest consultants billed the clients millions.

In the negligence category, we were recently involved in a case where an investigation of two groundwater aquifers was required. When installing the groundwater monitoring wells for the mandated site study, the prior consultant negligently cross-contaminated the clean lower aquifer with water from another aquifer.

In some instances, we have recommended the filing of an action directly against a consultant or environmental contractor who has perpetrated a fraud against a client or who has negligently performed his duties. Obviously, the decision to file such an action should not be taken lightly. In California, an attorney who brings an action against an engineering consultant must file a certificate of merit in support of the complaint as an extra safety measure.[41] The attorney must consult with and obtain an opinion from a professional engineer licensed in the same discipline as the consultant or engineer to be

41. Cal. Code Civ. Proc. § 411.35.

sued. The professional engineer who is consulted must be knowledgeable in the relevant issues involved in the action, and the attorney pursuing the action must certify under oath the belief that there is a reasonable and meritorious cause for the filing of the complaint against the consultant or engineer.

Be wary of a consultant with the designation of "R.E.A." or "E.I.T." after their name. Registered Environmental Assessor (R.E.A.) was a designation given by the California Department of Toxic Substances Control (DTSC) to identify and register environmental assessment and compliance professionals.[42] As of July 1, 2012, the REA Program no longer exists.

"E.I.T." is certification as an Engineer-in-Training, the first step required under California law towards becoming licensed as a professional engineer. An individual with an E.I.T. certification is not a professional state-licensed engineer in the state of California or anywhere in the United States. To be certified as an E.I.T., an applicant need only have three or more years of either postsecondary (college-level) engineering education, engineering-related work experience, or a combination of both, and have passed the NCEES Fundamentals of Engineering (FE) exam. Traditionally this test is taken by graduating senior engineering college students. In fact, an E.I.T. need not even have graduated, so long as the requirements for the certification were met.

Fortunately, rogue consultants are rare. Don't assume that just because remediation is costly that you have been duped. Environmental investigations and cleanups can be expensive even when they are properly performed. As such, before you launch your ship into uncharted waters by suing your consultant, we make several suggestions:

- You should retain an environmental lawyer and an environmental consultant of your own.
- Your environmental counsel and environmental consultant should carefully check the curriculum vitae of the environmental consultant to be sued and should investigate the various consulting firms with which the environmental consultant in question is and has been associated.
- You should give close scrutiny to the various approvals and sign-

42. The California Registered Environmental Assessor program was voluntary and consisted of two levels: REA I and REA II. An REA I was for professionals with 5 years of experience performing environmental assessments relating to hazardous substances and/or hazardous waste management (along with other requirements). An REA II is for professionals who also have experience in subsurface investigations and site mitigation.

offs between the consultant in question and all subcontractors and regulators.

- You should check and cross-check all pertinent regulations governing the remedial activities performed—to determine whether the consultant followed such regulations.
- To the extent that other remedial alternatives existed for the remedial investigation or cleanup which was pursued, you should give careful attention to whether these other alternatives were discussed and considered by the consultant and the consultant's client.

Boots on the Ground

The authors have each encountered situations when Regional Water Board staff engineers have not communicated with clients for years . . . literally years. After five years, one water board staff engineer called to ask where the quarterly groundwater monitoring data was. We said we had not heard from them in five years. He repeated the question. We eventually complied with his request. Had we ignored his request the Board could have issued an Administrative Compliance Order on Consent ("AOC") pursuant to the authority vested in the EPA by Section 309(a) of the federal Clean Water Act.

4. Is Groundwater Cleanup Necessary?

The Los Angeles Regional Board has sample steps for determining whether groundwater monitoring and/or groundwater cleanup are necessary.

Reproduced on the next page is a table from the Los Angeles Regional Board's Interim

Site Assessment and Cleanup Guidebook (Volume I: Assessment and Cleanup Guidance), dated February 1995. Their home page is www.waterboards.ca.gov/losangeles/.

The Los Angeles Regional Board, and presumably the other regional boards, sometimes require groundwater monitoring only and not groundwater cleanup when the contamination is minimal or relatively confined. Monitoring only, without cleanup, may be recommended where the groundwater beneath a site either has not yet been impacted by the soil contamination present at the site or the groundwater aquifer is not of beneficial use.

STEPS	CRITERIA TO CONSIDER
Consult with Regional Board staff and consider the listed criteria before deciding whether GROUND WATER CLEANUP or MONITORING is necessary	• Depth to the soil contaminants and groundwater. *Nature and extent of groundwater contamination. *Hydraulic properties of aquifer. • Type of soil contaminants and levels. • Compare groundwater contaminant levels to MCLs and ALs [i.e., "action levels"]. • Potential of the contaminants to migrate. • Location of drinking water wells in the area. • BAT [i.e., "best available technology"]. • Cleanup and monitoring costs. • Groundwater quality in nearby wells. • Regional cleanup/control strategies.
GROUNDWATER MONITORING may be appropriate in lieu of GROUNDWATER CLEANUP	• Compare groundwater contaminant levels to MCLs and ALs. • Groundwater quality in nearby wells. • Regional cleanup/control strategies.

In addition to the criteria listed above, the groundwater gradient may also be important to determine whether other parties in proximity to the site contributed to the contamination at issue. The groundwater or hydraulic gradient is simply a measure of the direction of underground groundwater flow, both horizontal and vertical, and may be highly variable. The groundwater gradient, or hydraulic gradient, determines the groundwater flow (direction of movement through groundwater) of any contaminants that are dissolved in or carried along with the groundwater. The groundwater flow direction could be the determining factor in whether you should be a party in an action involving a contamination problem or whether offsite sources contributed to, or may even be wholly responsible for, the contamination onsite. The groundwater gradient may frequently change within short distances and over short periods of based on

- groundwater pumping from subsurface aquifers,
- seasonal rainfall, or
- other water irrigation uses.

For instance, it is not uncommon for a manufacturer that has never used a particular hazardous substance to be sued for contributing to a contamination problem on a neighboring property. Diligent inquiry and technical investigation may later reveal that the client is simply stuck in the middle, and the contamination problem was caused by an unrelated up-gradient source. In other words, assume that the groundwater flows downstream, from an upstream property down through your property. Obviously, your property may be a passive conduit for contamination traveling even further downstream, contaminating the property immediately downstream of your property. Yet the contamination originated from an up-gradient, upstream source. If litigation ensues, but the up-gradient source has not been identified as a potentially responsible party (PRP), you may need to bring that party into the lawsuit to avoid being left holding the bag.

C. Is There a Vapor Intrusion Problem?[43]

We were living in a relatively simple world in 2004, when we came out with the first edition of this book. In terms of liability concerns, the soil or the groundwater (or both) could be contaminated. We had a clear systematic approach to determine how to analyze the matter, investigate the mess, and then clean it up.

That was before vapor intrusion ("VI") became an environmental and regulatory concern. Now, the "sick building" syndrome associated with toxic mold has been far

---

43. This section was contributed by Robert Ettinger. Mr. Ettinger is a Senior Principal Environmental Scientist with Geosyntec Consultants based in California with more than 20 years of professional experience focused on soil vapor extraction system design, vapor emission estimation, and subsurface contaminant vapor migration to indoor air. His contributions to advancing the state of the practice began with his co-authorship of the Johnson and Ettinger (1991) algorithm for evaluating subsurface contaminant vapor intrusion to indoor air. During the past 15 years, additional contributions have been made through field investigations and modeling evaluations on subsurface contaminant vapor intrusion to indoor air. His work is widely cited by regulators and industry groups as the reference point for beginning vapor intrusion assessments.

surpassed by what damage, real or hypothetical, volatile organic chemicals ("VOCs")—such as PCE, TCE, and others—can do to the health of people who either inhabit or occupy buildings in close proximity to where hazardous chemical releases have occurred. First, one needs to determine whether a hazardous release in soil has permeated upward in the soil column. Next, one needs to determine whether these chemicals made their way through vapor barriers or concrete. Then, one needs to determine whether these chemicals are off-gassing from contaminated groundwater in the subsurface. Is the process of chemical off-gassing contributing to the problem, or the primary cause of it? There are various other sources of VOCs in indoor air (e.g., background outdoor air contamination, use of common chemical products within the building, or vapor entry through improperly sealed sewer utility lines) that can impact indoor air quality and can make it very difficult to figure out whether we have encountered a major problem.

The latest EPA guidance came out in 2015 and was entitled "OSWER Technical Guide for Assessing and Mitigating the Vapor Intrusion Pathway from Subsurface Vapor Sources to Indoor Air." Let us try to explain what this document means.

Vapor intrusion (VI) is a *technical* term defined as the migration of chemical vapors from the subsurface into buildings. It is a frequent health problem at contaminated sites. If uncontrolled, chemical vapors can migrate into buildings and pose a risk to human health. Vapor migration emanating from the subsurface, through building foundations and within buildings is complex and influenced by many natural and human-caused factors. These factors can include climate (e.g., temperature, pressure, precipitation); building conditions (e.g., foundation type, status, age, and size); and active building systems like heating, ventilation, and air conditioning (HVAC) operation.

The VI conceptual model provides a framework, or template, to describe the transport mechanisms that influence the migration of VOCs in the subsurface to indoor air. As depicted in Figure A below, the basic vapor intrusion conceptual model for a groundwater (chemical) source assumes volatilization of chemicals from groundwater into soil vapor, then migration of these vapors through soil toward the surface, and then entry of these vapors into the building through existing cracks/openings in the building foundation.

VOCs present in groundwater at the water table interface, or in soil above the water table, will partition (i.e., volatilize) from groundwater, based on chemical-specific properties and their concentration at the water table. Chemicals that are present below the water table depth will not partition into soil vapor. As a result, measurements of VOCs below the water table do not reflect the source of chemicals that may volatilize into unsaturated zone soils.

VOCs migrate through soil by a process called diffusion, wherein chemicals naturally move from areas of higher concentrations to areas of lower concentrations. As a result of the diffusion transport, chemical concentrations near the ground surface are lower than those at the source or water table interface. Practically speaking, this means that chemical concentrations in the soil are lower as the distance from the source increases.

Chemicals in soil vapor can enter the building structure through cracks in the building foundation or gaps around utility penetrations. The soil vapor entry into the structure can typically be driven by wind effects, stack effects (caused by heating within the building), or mechanical ventilation (e.g., bathroom fans) that induce a slight depressurization of the building.

Chemicals entering the building will disperse in indoor air because of building ventilation. The building ventilation may be natural (i.e., windows) or mechanical.

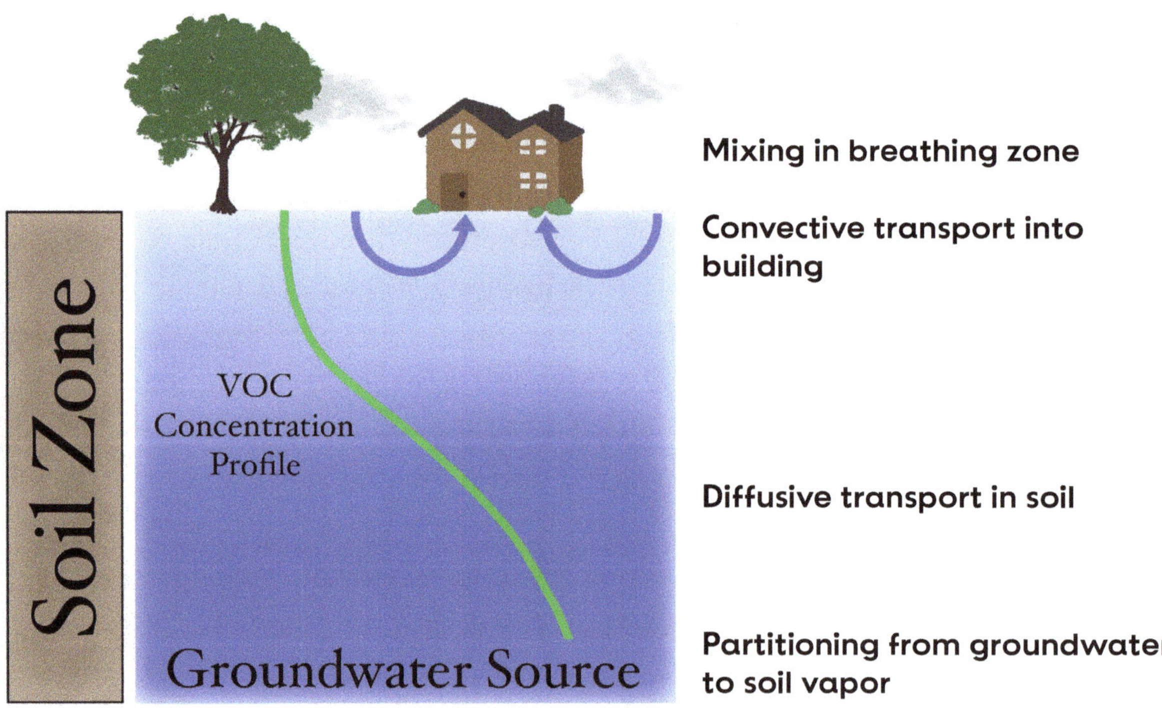

Other factors can affect the potential significance of the vapor intrusion pathway or influence the interpretation of site investigation data:

- Lateral separation: the primary direction of soil vapor diffusion is upward. Lateral diffusive migration of VOCs in soil will be limited. Typically, vapor intrusion evaluations are limited to buildings within 100 feet of the subsurface source.[44]

- Background sources: VOCs are often detected in indoor air due to background sources of chemicals unrelated to subsurface impacts.[45] Background sources may include building materials, household activities, or consumer products used in the buildings. A more detailed investigation (often called a multiple-lines-of-evidence evaluation) is typically necessary to assess whether chemicals detected in indoor air are due to vapor intrusion or background sources.
- Natural biodegradation of chemicals in the soil.
- Presence of preferential pathways.

There are several California EPA guidance documents that may be considered in the evaluation of the vapor intrusion pathway:

- DTSC, 2011: Final Guidance for the Evaluation and Mitigation of Subsurface Vapor Intrusion to Indoor Air (Vapor Intrusion Guidance)
- DTSC, 2011: Vapor Intrusion Mitigation Advisory
- DTSC, 2012: Vapor Intrusion Public Participation Advisory
- CalEPA, 2015: Advisory-Active Soil Gas Investigations
- CalEPA, 2020. San Francisco Bay Regional Water Quality Control Board's
- Supplemental Guidance: Screening and Evaluating Vapor Intrusion (Draft for Public Comments)

The discussion which follows is intended to open the door for you so that you can begin to ask the right questions to get answers when dealing with contaminated property. First, and most importantly, you cannot do this alone. You will need an experienced consultant. Evaluation of this chemical pathway requires knowledge of chemical movement through soil and groundwater, building mechanics, and human health risk assessments. Consequently,

44. EPA Office of Solid Waste and Emergency Response, OSWER Technical Guide for Assessing and Mitigating the Vapor Intrusion Pathway from Subsurface Vapor Sources to Indoor Air. OSWER Publication 9200.2-154, June 2015; Interstate Technology and Regulatory Council Technical and Regulatory Guidance, Vapor Intrusion Pathway: A Practical Guideline. January 2007.

45. EPA Office of Solid Waste and Emergency Response, OSWER Technical Guide for Assessing and Mitigating the Vapor Intrusion Pathway from Subsurface Vapor Sources to Indoor Air. OSWER Publication 9200.2-154, June 2015.

multiple technical resources, including environmental geologists, environmental engineers, building engineers, toxicologists, and/or public health experts may be needed to assist you with a vapor intrusion evaluation.

Typically, a 4-step process is used to evaluate the VI pathway:

- Preliminary screening
- Site investigation
- Risk-based decision making
- Mitigation and/or long-term monitoring

Preliminary screening is an initial step to ensure that immediate health or safety risks are not present and to assess the presence of chemicals that could potentially present a VI concern. Limited data are typically available at this point, and site soil vapor and groundwater data are compared to regulatory agencies' recommended conservative screening levels to assess whether a site-specific vapor intrusion investigation is warranted.

Site investigations typically begin with collection of exterior soil vapor samples near structures to assess whether indoor samples should be collected. If near-building exterior soil vapor concentrations exceed regulatory screening levels, then indoor air sampling will often be conducted. (However, this may not be feasible for redevelopment sites where there are no buildings, or where existing buildings will be torn down prior to redevelopment.) Considerable planning is required prior to conducting VI investigations at a site, to ensure adequate sampling addressing temporal and spatial variability, avoid interference due to background sources of volatile chemicals, and coordination with site owners and tenants.

In some cases, specialized investigation techniques may be used to resolve the uncertainty associated with data variability and background interferences. The data collected during the site VI investigation are used to develop a VI Site-Conceptual Model that summarizes the sources, migration pathways, and receptors that may be affected by this pathway.

The *risk-based decision-making* process involves the review of the data collected, VI site conceptual model, assessment of potential short-term and long-term risks to building occupants, and uncertainties in the data evaluation to assess whether remediation and/or VI-mitigation is necessary.

Mitigation and/or long-term monitoring may be implemented to prevent long-term indoor air exposures that pose unacceptable health risks. The most common VI mitigation approach is to install a sub-slab depressurization system. However, the selected mitigation approach will depend on site conditions (e.g., vapor concentrations, building construction). Sub-slab depressurization systems are often used to address vapor intrusion of naturally occurring radon in some parts of the country, so the application of this technology is well-known. In some cases, long-term monitoring may be used to ensure that the VI conditions do not change over time in a way that would adversely impact building occupants.

Petroleum Release Sites

Petroleum releases from underground storage tanks (USTs) must be evaluated for vapor intrusion using the State Water Board's Resolution 2012-0062, Low-Threat Underground Storage Tank (UST) Case Closure Policy (LTCP), adopted November 6, 2012 (State Water Board, 2012b).

The conceptual model for VI of petroleum hydrocarbons (petroleum vapor intrusion, PVI) indicates that natural biodegradation of hydrocarbons in the vadose zone mitigates the VI pathway.[46] A simplified conceptual model for PVI is shown above.

Provided there is a sufficient flux (i.e., movement) of oxygen from the atmosphere to the subsurface region beneath building structures, aerobic biodegradation of petroleum compounds will naturally mitigate the vapor intrusion pathway. This has been documented in numerous site investigations summarized by EPA[47] and this factor is commonly used to develop bioattenuation[48] factors for PVI assessments. The San Francisco Bay Regional Water Quality Control Board (SFBRWQCB) recommends a bioattenuation factor of 1,000 for sites where bioattenuation is demonstrated. Additional data collection to demonstrate that subsurface conditions are conducive for aerobic biodegradation typically consists of characterizing the oxygen content in shallow soil vapor samples to show that sufficient

46. Interstate Technology and Regulatory Council, Petroleum Vapor Intrusion: Fundamentals of Screening, Investigation, and Management, October 2014; EPA Office of Underground Storage Tanks, Evaluation of Empirical Data to Support Soil Vapor Intrusion Screening Criteria for Petroleum Hydrocarbon Compounds, January 2013.

47. EPA Office of Underground Storage Tanks, Evaluation of Empirical Data to Support Soil Vapor Intrusion Screening Criteria for Petroleum Hydrocarbon Compounds, January 2013.

48. Bioattenuation is the process where pollutants [like petroleum hydrocarbons] are transformed to less harmful forms or immobilized in the soil. Such transformation and immobilization processes are largely due to biodegradation by microorganisms and to some extent by the reactions with naturally occurring chemicals and sorption in the soil.

oxygen is present in the subsurface to permit biodegradation. California regulatory guidance documents recommend that an oxygen concentration of 2–4% by volume is sufficient to maintain an aerobic condition to mitigate the vapor intrusion pathway.[49] These oxygen concentrations support the use of the bioattenuation factor, which results in screening levels that are 1,000 times higher than default levels for chlorinated VOCs.

49. Interstate Technology and Regulatory Council, *Petroleum Vapor Intrusion: Fundamentals of Screening, Investigation, and Management*, October 2014.

Chapter III:
How Do You Get a Handle on It?

Your environmental counsel cannot function without reading environmental reports. Counsel must know—in context—what issues and technical subject matter the various types of environmental reports need to contain. There may be subjects required by the appropriate regulatory agencies having jurisdiction over your specific environmental investigation and remediation. Your counsel may be well on his or her way to determining what the pertinent regulatory agency requires, but sometimes the essential *issues* are either ignored or not sufficiently addressed in the report. Your counsel must be able to tell you if the cleanup for which you have purported liability was inappropriately or ineffectively conducted.

For instance, it is not uncommon to find that the reports prepared by a consultant plainly indicate that regulatory requirements were not met or, more importantly, that either a "no action" approach or a more cost-effective alternative was not proposed, considered, or weighed as a possible alternative by a prior consultant. It should be noted that the selection of a cost-effective remedy is a requirement in order to show substantial compliance with the National Contingency Plan (the NCP, discussed below).[50] Under California state law, for example, consultants must consider the actual projected cost of each cleanup when weighing alternative cleanup scenarios. Yet, practically speaking, cost is never a factor while a remediation approach is weighed by regulatory agencies. Unfortunately, you don't get any points for being cost-conscious. The goal of the regulators is to clean up a site. The cost is your burden.

After analyzing the environmental report in question, your counsel must decide what

50. See 40 C.F.R. § 300.430(e)(7) (1995).

further investigation is necessary, including making appropriate Freedom of Information Act (FOIA, pronounced "foi-yah") requests to the EPA or public records requests to state or local regulatory agencies.

A. Requirements for Cost Recovery

If a CERCLA lawsuit—that is, a federal Superfund lawsuit—has been filed against you pursuant to the joint and several liability provisions, or the contribution provisions of CERCLA, STOP READING THIS AND FIND AN ATTORNEY, IMMEDIATELY. Believe us. If litigation is underway, it is one minute to midnight, and you will need help. This is no longer a "do it yourself to save money" exercise. You need to act smartly—Now. Take a deep breath, close this book, and start making phone calls to get appropriate help.

If the plaintiff is a private party (not the EPA or a local regulatory agency), they must establish a prima facie case of liability against you as owner or operator of the site, or against someone who has arranged for the offsite disposal of hazardous waste.[51] They will also need to establish that their cleanup actions were necessary and consistent with the federal National Contingency Plan (NCP) as a condition for recovery in a CERCLA private cost recovery action.[52]

If the plaintiff is the federal government, the standard is whether the costs incurred by the government in the cleanup were not *inconsistent* with the NCP. This is a lower standard for the government to meet, since the burden is on the defendant to prove that any of the federal government's costs were incurred for matters *inconsistent* with the NCP.

In a private party lawsuit, however, the plaintiff has the burden of showing consistency with the NCP as a part of its prima facie case. Under the 1990 NCP, actions taken by a private party to clean up a site will be considered consistent with the NCP if the actions are in "substantial compliance" with the applicable requirements of the NCP and result in

---

51. "To establish a prima facie case of liability in a CERCLA cost recovery action, a plaintiff must prove: (1) that the site in question is a 'facility' as defined in §9601(9); (2) that the defendant is a responsible person under §9607(a); (3) that a release or threatened release of a hazardous substance has occurred; and, (4) that the release or threatened release has caused the plaintiff to incur response costs." *Amoco Oil Co. v. Borden, Inc.* (5th Cir. 1989) 889 F.2d 664, 668; *Ascon Properties, Inc. v. Mobil Oil Co.* (9th Cir. 1989) 866 F.2d 1149, 1152-1153.

52. See 40 C.F.R. § 300.700(c)(3)(i)

a CERCLA-quality cleanup.[53] To be consistent with the 1990 NCP, the reports generated by the party conducting the site cleanup must contain certain specific elements. In addition, the various written reports prepared must also follow a certain sequence of investigation.[54] If the cleanup was conducted under state law, your environmental counsel should be careful to compare the prepared reports against the guidelines, requirements and protocols articulated by the specific state agency having jurisdiction over the cleanup. It should be noted that there is no concept of a legacy exception to the rules (i.e., "grandfathering"). Simply stated, a legacy exception is a provision in which an old rule continues to apply to existing situations, while a new rule will apply to all future cases. In environmental law, the rules change frequently. If the rules change today, *the new rules* are now in effect. The fact that your client was in compliance yesterday is old news. He must be in compliance with the current rules. So, if you are reviewing the rules, they must always be current.

B. Types of Environmental Reports

1. Phase I Environmental Site Assessment (Initial Site Evaluation)

This report is normally prepared in conjunction with a real property transfer by either the buyer or seller, or as part of an application for a real estate loan or for refinancing a loan on an existing parcel. A proper Phase I investigation comports with due diligence requirements to enable a mortgage lender to determine whether the subject site is contaminated and/or reduced in value in any way. Simply stated, can the site be used for collateral?

The Phase I investigation does not involve any proactive site investigations except for a site walkover. There is no intrusive sampling. It does not include the taking of any soil or groundwater samples on the property. No dirt is disturbed, no shovels are used. It is merely a "snapshot" of the property at a specific point in time. It is also a record of the land use at the property, including surrounding properties. This report is used to determine whether there are any historic or current potential sources of contamination, such as accidental spill events, prior tenants, or prior uses that would justify closer investigation. If it is determined

---

53. "Response costs are considered consistent with the NCP 'if the action, when evaluated as a whole, is in substantial compliance' with it." *City of Colton v. Am. Promotional Events, Inc.*, 614 F.3d 998, 1003 (9th Cir. 2010); See 40 C.F.R. § 300.700(c)(3)(i)

54. See 40 C.F.R. § 300.430 (1990).

that the property is potentially contaminated or that potential sources of contamination exist in or around the property, a further, more intrusive investigation will be required. This additional, subsequent investigation is called a Phase II investigation. It will likely involve geotechnical activity, including soil borings and chemical sample analyses of soil and/or groundwater.

Phase I reports are usually written to comply with standards from the American Society of Testing Materials (ASTM).The current standard for the Phase I Environmental Site Assessment Process is identified as E1527-97. A shorter, less complete version of this standard is the ASTM Standard Practice for Environmental Site Assessments: Transaction Screen Process E1528-96.

A consultant performing a Phase I investigation may ask the following questions:[55]

- Can you obtain records of former tenants, leases, correspondence reflecting rental agreements / tenancies, periods of occupancy, types of activities, etc.?
- Can you obtain copies of insurance policies of former tenants and owners, going back historically as far as possible?
- What were previous land uses, periods of activities, owners, chain-of-title reports?
- What are adjacent land uses surrounding the site? What is the history of these land uses?
- Has a survey been performed of the existing state and federal lists to determine the incidence of violations, or listing within the general vicinity? When were the computer-generated files last updated?
- Is the site located within a 100-year flood plain?[56]

---

55. The ASTM (American Society of Testing Materials) has promulgated Standards on Environmental Site Assessments for Commercial Real Estate: from ASTM standards E1527-97 (Standard Practice for Environmental Site Assessments: Phase 1 Environmental Site Assessment Process) and E1528-96 (Standard Practice for Environmental Site Assessments: Transaction Screen Process.) It should be noted that the questions in this text are less imposing than the ASTM screening questions and may actually garner more information than the ASTM questions which, nevertheless, are being used by most financial institutions

56. Flood Plain means any land area susceptible to inundation by floodwaters from any source. 100-year Flood Plain is the area adjoining a river, stream, or watercourse covered by water in the event of a 100-year flood. 100-year Flood (also called the Base Flood) is a flood having a one percent chance of being equaled or exceeded in magnitude in any given year. Contrary to popular belief, it is not a flood occurring once every 100 years.

- Are previous environmental studies available for asbestos or PCBs?[57]
- Are there any underground storage tanks ("USTs") or above-ground storage tanks ("ASTs") on site? Have there ever been? What did they contain? Were the ASTs and/or USTs removed? If so, when?
- Do any current or past tenants have EPA Generator Numbers? Why?
- Do any tenants have any permits for wastewater discharge? Are the permits current? Have there been any violations?
- Have any hazardous spills occurred on site? Have the incidents been reported to the local fire department or other appropriate agency?
- Do the site tenant(s) generate, store, or treat hazardous wastes (including waste oil) as defined under the federal Resource Conservation and Recovery Act (RCRA)?
- Are wastes disposed of as dictated by or outlined in the federal or California state manifest system?
- Are pesticides stored or used on site?
- Has asbestos ever been removed? When, by whom, and why?
- Have present or former tenants on site or at adjacent or neighboring properties ever received notification of involvement as a Potentially Responsible Party (PRP) at a state or federal Superfund site?
- Are there parts cleaning stations associated with maintenance activities on site? What type and volume of solvents are used?
- Are there air compressors or cooling towers with blow down?
- Are there chillers on site that use Freon?

If a consultant is tasked with writing a Phase I report, some of the data may not be available in a time frame to suit your purposes. Public records requests for data to local city or county authorities sometimes cannot be completed until months after a written request has been made. Much historic data on underground tanks, for example, are still only kept in paper form, in file cabinets.

The consultant will have to answer the preceding questions to determine if all po-

---

57. According to the U.S. Agency for Toxic Substances and Disease Registry (ATSDR), polychlorinated biphenyls (PCBs) are a group of synthetic organic chemicals that can cause a number of different harmful effects. There are no known natural sources of PCBs in the environment. Once in the environment, PCBs do not readily break down in soil and may stay in the soil for months or years. PCBs, historically, were a major constituent of most hydraulic fluids (trade name: Aroclor) which were routinely used in hydraulic lifts before 1977. Both the EPA and the International Agency for Research on Cancer (IARC) have determined that PCBs are probably carcinogenic in humans. See http://www.epa.gov/pcb.

tential sources of onsite contamination have been located and identified to confirm the absence or presence of onsite pollution.

Typical potential sources of pollution include:

- above/underground tanks;
- existing sewer lines or known leaks from clay pipe sewer lines;
- contaminated soil;
- septic tanks or cesspools;
- vapor degreasers;
- paint booths;
- percolation sumps;
- illegal or unpermitted disposal or dumping;
- any structure containing and/or transporting chemicals, wastes, etc.;
- defined hazardous waste storage or drum storage areas;
- chemical spills;
- clarifiers—whose closures are usually not regulated;
- any underground piping;
- storm water runoff;
- landfills;
- toxic pits;
- contaminated runoff;
- leach fields;
- subsurface concrete vaults; or
- activities on neighboring properties.

Pursuant to California State Board Resolution 92-49, the following site information or relevant evidence can be used to assist anyone who is attempting to identify the absence or presence of potential sources of contamination on a property:

- Any historical information concerning chemical, waste, solvent, gasoline, etc. usage and storage can assist in establishing whether hazardous substances were used and discharged into the onsite soil. Descriptions of business or manufacturing operations (e.g., solvent manufacture) may help to clarify usage and storage practices.
- Your environmental consultant should conduct an onsite visit to visually spot potential sources and/or discharges to soil. Don't underes-

timate the value of an onsite visit—there is no substitute for "kicking dirt."

- Your consultant should review appropriate historical photographic archives and maps depicting the locations of former potential sources (e.g., above-ground tanks) particularly if (a) the facility no longer exists; (b) the facility has been modified in any way (use of a stereoscope viewer with historic aerial photographs can aid even the untrained eye); (c) use of the land or buildings has changed; (d) neighboring properties have been developed; or (e) heavy rains or flooding have changed either surface runoff patterns or channelization.
- Your consultant should contact city planning departments to obtain and study groundwater quality data obtained from nearby sites dating from previous construction. Such data might also be available from Environmental Impact Reports (EIRs) required under the California Environmental Quality Act (CEQA). Existing geotechnical data is available on the Geotracker (operated by the California State Water Board) and Envirostor (operated by the California Department of Toxic Substances Control) websites. Your consultant should determine (a) if groundwater quality has been impacted under the site or adjacent properties; (b) whether activities on the subject property may have contributed to the problem; or (c) if other properties have the potential to contribute to or cause problems on the client's site.
- A chain-of-title search should be performed on the site, usually spanning a minimum of 40 years. Phase I reports may be perceived as legally inadequate without the 40-year historic title search. You will want to know who previously owned your parcel and perhaps neighboring parcels.

CASE STUDY 6:
Phase I Reports from Up Close

Phase 1 reports are an essential tool when buying real estate—but there are some issues to keep a close eye on. This is a subject that can be squishy.

First, make sure that the report was written to comply with the latest ASTM standard. This sounds obvious, but it's easy to miss. On November 1, 2021, the American Society for Testing and Materials (ASTM) Committee on Environmental Assessment, Risk Management and Corrective Action (ASTM Committee E-50) approved a new standard for conducting Phase I Environmental Site Assessments (ESAs). The new standard, known as "E1527-27—Standard Practice for Environmental Site Assessments: Phase I Environmental Site Assessment Process," made significant modifications to the previous ASTM Phase I Standard Practice (E1527-13) that environmental professionals (EPs) had been using to perform Phase I ESAs for the preceding years. The standard is only available for purchase directly from the ASTM—each digital copy is numbered and identifies the purchaser.

The goal of writing an ASTM E1527 Phase I ESA is to identify the confirmed presence, likely presence, or a material threat of the presence of hazardous substances or petroleum products at a real property, also known as a "Recognized Environmental Condition" (REC). The ASTM E1527 Standard defines what constitutes "good commercial and customary practice for conducting an environmental site assessment of a parcel of commercial real estate in the United States of America with respect to the range of contaminants within the scope of [CERCLA, 42 U.S.C. § 9601] and petroleum products."

The previous ASTM E1527-13 Standard was incorporated by reference into rules promulgated by the federal Environmental Protection Agency (EPA) (known as the "All Appropriate Inquiry" [AAI] rule) to obtain protection from liability for contamination under CERCLA.

On one occasion, we were asked to review a recent ASTM E1527 Phase I ESA. It only has a useful shelf life of 180 days prior to the date of acquisition of a property, or otherwise up to one year, if five specific components of the report have been updated (interviews, searches for recorded environmental cleanup liens, review of government records, site reconnaissance of the subject property, and a declaration from the Environmental Professional).

The report we reviewed compiled data that was consistent with the then-current ASTM Standard E1527-13–Standard Practice for Environmental Site Assessments: Phase I Environmental Site Assessment Process. It met the criteria for checking all the various avenues of inquiry. The data was sufficient in our opinion to be acceptable to a lender. There were no "Recognized Environmental Conditions" as defined in the ASTM standard. Yet, in the conclusion to the Phase 1, the consultant defined the need for necessary environmental cleanup activities based upon "environmental issues"–the consultant's own term of art–which neither appeared nor were referenced anywhere in the ASTM standard at the time the Phase 1 was prepared. The report then went on to describe these "environmental issues" of concern and the need to remediate parts of the site based upon the "environmental issues" the consultant had defined.

We explained to the client that the need for additional work on the site was fallacious and not based upon the evidence. It appeared that the consultant was simply making a case to perform additional costly work on the site by defining "environmental issues" as though compliance with this made-up term was equivalent to acceptance of the ASTM Standard's criteria. The data in the report simply did not support this conclusion. The applicable ASTM standard for acceptance had been met. This situation had the appearance of unclean hands, in that the recommendation of additional required geologic investigations appeared motivated to benefit the company writing the report rather than to fulfil the ASTM standard. To avoid these sorts of issues, you may want to consider using two different consultants: one to write a Phase 1 report and another to perform any needed investigation or remediation on the property.

Another Phase 1 misunderstanding:

A client had requested a refinance from their bank to lower the interest rate on their existing loan with the same bank. The bank already had the loan; it was seasoned and there were no changes in use or any other relevant material changes. Yet the lender denied the loan refinance–the bank wanted a new Phase I. Why? Well, the justification for the request was based upon an "assigned Site Reassessment status" by US EPA on an adjoining property.

What could this mean? The bank had done a quick document review of existing governmental files and come across the term. To the bank, this meant some sinister (or at least unknown) activity had occurred next door. The bank didn't like the sound of a change of "assigned Site Reassessment status"–it sounded like something had changed for the worse. This triggered the bank's request for a new Phase I. The client was upset–this was supposed to be a plain, vanilla refinance.

We knew the property. It had been a retail center for at least 15 years–no hazardous waste, no chemicals, just paper goods. The term that spooked the bank was evidence that there was any activity. We researched available public documentation from the US EPA database. After reviewing the available documents, we determined that the US EPA had merely done a "windshield" survey of the site–a drive-by looksee by an EPA staffer. The purpose of the drive-by site review was to confirm that the site no longer had to be in included in EPA's database of contaminated properties. This type of activity is part of US EPA protocol to remove a property from the CERLCIS list, to confirm that the site does not require further site assessment. The site even had a No Further Action (NFA) status. Remediation activities on the adjoining site that had warranted review had long since been completed. The site was headed for the EPA's version of the dead letter office. A letter to the lender cleared up the issue and the loan was refinanced.

2. Phase II (Preliminary Site Assessment)

The goal of a Phase II assessment, also known as a preliminary site assessment or site investigation, is to determine if any unauthorized release has historically occurred at the site because of suspicions raised by the Phase I investigation. Other goals of the Phase II assessment are to (1) identify PRPs and (2) to collect preliminary information on the nature and extent of the contamination.[58]

---

58. See, e.g., 40 C.F.R. § 300.420(b)(1) (1995); California Regional Water Quality Control Board, Los Angeles

A soil gas (i.e., soil vapor) survey is one screening method which can be used during a preliminary site assessment. It is a method to investigate the existence of potential petroleum hydrocarbon or chlorinated solvent contamination in shallow soils over a large area. This type of survey is relatively inexpensive and has many uses. It can be used to determine whether petroleum hydrocarbons or chlorinated solvents like TCE and PCE exist in the soil, obtain a rough idea of their concentrations and extent, and help determine if and where additional soil sampling work should be performed. Long hollow steel rods (like elongated drinking straws) are pounded into the soil at regular intervals over the site to be tested. A syringe is then inserted within the tube, and a volume of air is extracted into the syringe for testing. Several samples can be taken with a single boring by extracting the contained air at different depths as the rod is pushed further and further into the soil

CRITICAL POINT: The soil vapor investigation process involves sampling air, not soil. Soil vapor analysis is not a substitute for soil (also called "soil matrix") sampling. If the soil vapor analysis discloses an area of concern, you must then follow up with proper soil sampling. Otherwise, you would not have validation that the soil vapor sample was testing the subsurface *soil*. Without a subsequent soil sample at the same location, you would not know if you had simply found a subsurface gas cloud—or contaminated soil. So, this is a screening tool to cover large sites to determine where further soil samples should be taken.

Soil sampling work plans should be developed in connection with a soil gas/vapor survey. Soil sampling will determine if soil contamination

- is above regulatory action levels,
- has impacted the site, or
- is capable of endangering or impacting groundwater quality beneath the site.

Again, using confirmatory soil sampling to validate soil vapor testing at the same locations used for soil vapor testing is very important. A positive soil vapor analysis does not necessarily indicate contaminated soil. For example, there may be contamination in the groundwater originating from a neighboring property. This neighboring contamination may be caused by volatile organic compounds like PCE or TCE which have traveled through the soil column, reached the groundwater, migrated to your site through the groundwater, and then moved upward through the soil column in the form of a "vapor cloud." This vapor cloud would cause a positive soil vapor reading for PCE or TCE when there is no

---

Region, *Self-Directed Process for The Investigation and Cleanup of Petroleum-Impacted Sites* (May 1994) § 4.1.

contamination in the soil matrix on your property (although there likely would be on the neighboring property). Therefore, again, without performing confirmatory soil sampling at the same location where soil vapor testing was performed, it cannot be accurately determined whether the soil is contaminated.

Sometimes, but not always, groundwater samples are taken. These samples could indicate evidence of contamination but could also show evidence of chemical contamination that has neither originated on your site nor resulted from your activities. For example, if there is evidence of BTEX gasoline constituents in the groundwater, and there is no history of gasoline usage on your property, the contaminants probably entered the groundwater from someone else's property.

3. Remedial Investigation (Complete Site Assessment)

The goals of the remedial investigation or complete site assessment are to

- fully define the sources and the vertical and lateral extent of the contaminant plume in the soil and groundwater,
- characterize the site geology and hydrogeology, and
- evaluate potential risks to public health and the environment.

Typically, a remedial investigation or complete site assessment report should include such elements as:

- a description of the site background, including a map of the site and its various structures, drawn to scale and showing all significant site features;
- identification and location of the contaminants and sources of contamination;
- a description of site specific and regional geology and hydrogeology;
- a complete delineation of the vertical and lateral extent of the soil and groundwater contamination, as identified through soil borings, groundwater monitoring wells, and the analytical data generated during this work; and
- data necessary to develop remedial cleanup options.

The site background section of the remedial investigation report will essentially reiterate—or copy—the Phase I report. But it may also include updated regulatory information not previously available.

The remedial investigation report should contain a site facility map. The map should identify locations of all potential sources of contamination (including underground and above-ground tanks, clarifiers, hazardous material storage areas, floor drains, onsite underground piping, and sewers). The map should be drawn to some identifiable scale. Site boundaries, important structures, and significant physical features of the site must be shown on the map, along with adjacent streets and properties. Use and ownership of adjacent properties should be described. In the sections of the report that deal with the testing of site soils and groundwater, the rationale should be explained for the number and location of soil borings, and the reasons for the proposed depth of each boring. Many state regulatory agencies require soil sampling and testing to be performed at every five feet of depth down to close to the water table. The report should characterize the groundwater gradient and the depth to groundwater across the various areas of the site. The rationale for where groundwater monitoring wells were installed should also be described.

The actual soil boring logs (usually attached as an appendix to the site characterization report, or to the report describing proposed remedial actions) will often seem too technical for the layman to review. Consequently, most site owners and attorneys will also overlook them as a source of data. Do not make this mistake! They can contain important information. The well logger or supervising geologist who oversees the soil borings will usually make notes on the standard boring log sheets in the field during the actual drilling. These notes can contain valuable information. For example, the well logger may note a petroleum odor (indicating the presence—or former presence—of gasoline or diesel fuel). Or perhaps a sweet pungent odor is noted in the well logs—this is usually associated with the presence of "perc" or tetracholorethylene, a solvent. These practical observations can be invaluable.

If groundwater has been contaminated, state law requires that a minimum of three groundwater monitoring wells be initially installed to determine the groundwater flow direction, hydraulic gradient (velocity), and aerial extent of the groundwater contamination. These wells have a prescribed pattern to their locations. At a minimum, two wells should be placed downgradient and one should be placed upgradient of the contamination source (in geologists' parlance, "one up and two down"). If the extent of the contamination or the offsite migration cannot be defined by three wells, additional wells must be installed to fully characterize the groundwater direction on your site. If you have faith in your consultant, have faith in your consultant. This is an art, not a science. Sometimes, the only "profound" conclusion which can be reached from the first round of soil or groundwater sampling is that the data is inconclusive. One more well, or, testing a few more data points could mean the difference between ignorance and knowledge. It's always cheaper in the long run to define the problem before you start solving it.

State and county permits are required for the installation of any groundwater monitoring wells. General standards for well construction, reconstruction, repair, or abandonment must comply, for example, with California Department of Water Resources Bulletin 74 81 and 74 90, and Chapter 16 Regulations, Section 2649.

4. Description of Existing Remediation Technologies[59]

There are many techniques used for site soil and groundwater remediation. Each has advantages and disadvantages. Some techniques involve removing the contaminants or the affected media from the ground. These are called "ex-situ." Others involve destroying the contaminants in the ground—these technologies are referred to as "in-situ." While air quality remediation is not directly described, please realize that consideration of air quality issues is an integral part of any site soil remediation plan. Some of the technologies described here cannot be used without permits from the local Air Quality Management District.

a. Excavation

Often the simplest and most complete way of removing contamination is to directly remove the contaminated soil and dispose of it off site. This can be costly and complicated, especially if buildings or other infrastructure are in the way. But excavation should always be the baseline approach that other remedies are compared against, in terms of cost and implementation, because it offers finality and is generally favored by regulatory agencies.

---

59. This section was authored by Jeremy Squire, PE, QSD, QISP, jeremysquire@murexenv.com. Mr. Squire is Vice President of Murex Environmental, Inc., an Irvine, California-based environmental engineering and consulting firm, and is a California-licensed civil and environmental engineer and an expert in site assessment, soil and groundwater remediation, and environmental litigation support. His team of engineers, geologists, and scientists support brownfield redevelopment projects, industrial site cleanup projects, and legal disputes involving hazardous materials contamination.

b. Soil Vapor Extraction (SVE)

This technique has been successful in the removal of volatile organic chemicals (VOCs) and non-aqueous phase liquids (NAPLs) in the unsaturated vadose zone (the vadose zone is the space just above the saturated zone—the water table, or aquifer). SVE applies a vacuum through piping and extraction wells to remove volatile chemicals from the subsurface. It is often the best remedy for larger or more diffuse source areas because it can be easily scaled up. Air sparging to treat groundwater may be used in conjunction with SVE, since the two are complementary.

c. Pump and Treat

Saturated soil zones contain groundwater in formations called aquifers. When contaminated groundwater is removed from the subsurface by pumping, it is often treated before it is discharged. Therefore, this method is referred to as pump-and-treat. This is the oldest and most traditional form of groundwater remediation. These systems pump contaminated groundwater out of the aquifer using pumping wells. The extracted water is then treated (i.e., cleaned up) above ground and either discharged to the storm drain or re-injected into the groundwater. This technology can be expensive—it takes many years and large volumes of water to remove the contaminants of concern.

d. Air Sparging

Air sparging is used for the remediation of volatile and/or biodegradable contamination from aquifers. This remediation technique introduces air bubbles into the saturated zone of an aquifer. Forcing air into the aquifer increases volatilization of contaminants from the saturated zone where the contaminants can then be removed with SVE. Most remediation techniques to clean up contaminated underground aquifers have relied on the movement and treatment of water, whereas air sparging relies upon the movement and treatment of air.

Air sparging, when used in conjunction with SVE, can also be effective in removing VOC contaminants from both the saturated and unsaturated zones. It can also stimulate biological degradation. Air sparging allows for the displacement of water-filled pores with sparged air, which induces mechanical mixing of the groundwater and enhances the rate of adsorbed and residual NAPL dissolution. Under normal conditions, there isn't much interface between air and subsurface contaminants. Air sparging can increase this contact time, thereby facilitating removal of adsorbed and dissolved VOCs.

Air sparging may also enhance biodegradation of petroleum contaminants. Through dissolved oxygen injection, air sparging induces aerobic biodegradation of many VOCs. With increased availability of oxygen, bioremediation activities accelerate remediation.

e. In-Situ Chemical Oxidation

Many contaminants are susceptible to being oxidized by strong bleaching agents, like ozone gas and potassium permanganate. Injecting these agents into an aquifer can destroy the contamination, leaving behind only oxygen gas and dissolved minerals. It takes closely spaced injections to treat the entire area, so it is sometimes not possible to perform chemical oxidation when the plume is too big, or when groundwater is deeper than 100 feet.

f. In-Situ Bioremediation

This is a technique that involves stimulating naturally occurring microorganisms in the subsurface by adding nutrients; it can also include introducing specially grown microbes into the site's aquifer to enhance the biological degradation of specific degradable organic contaminants. This process must be used expertly to be cost effective. In the right hands and appropriate environment, it can be prudent and significantly reduce remediation manpower costs. In the wrong hands, it can lead to delay, additional costs, and . . . yes, disaster.

g. Natural Attenuation

Some contaminants, especially when the chemicals exhibit lower or diffuse concentrations, can be degraded by the environment without intervention. The mechanisms of dilution, dispersion, abiotic and biotic degradation, and evaporation have the combined capacity to steadily lower contaminant concentrations over time; this is called "natural attenuation." It is an accepted method by which the end, or "polishing" step of cleanup is accomplished on most sites. For instance, if you have performed SVE and air sparging, and the residual concentrations are low but not zero, it is generally acceptable to leave the remainder to be naturally attenuated. Consultants must provide evidence that this will occur for it to be acceptable, such as by monitoring for a year or two and demonstrating that a downward trend will continue.

h. Monitoring

Groundwater monitoring programs are usually needed to verify the effectiveness of cleanup projects. Monitoring the cleanup allows the operator to make adjustments to the system in response to changes in subsurface conditions and determine when the project may be coming to an end.

A major component of any remediation system or approach is determining when the soil and groundwater are clean enough. The contaminant cleanup levels are usually established under the federal Safe Drinking Water Act unless local laws are more stringent. Consultants often perform risk analysis (estimating the risk to human health and natural resources) to demonstrate that enough work has been done.

After you've done all that you can and spent all the money that you've been asked to spend, you must wait. How long? For as long as the regulatory agencies tell you to. Monitoring may be required for up to three to five years—usually quarterly (every three months). Just say thank you; they're done with you. It's a small price to pay for finishing the process.

5. Feasibility Study (Corrective Action Plan)

In a CERCLA-driven Superfund case, this particular report is called a Feasibility Study, or "FS."[60] In a state law pollution case, where one of the RWQCBs (Regional Water Quality Control Boards) may have jurisdiction over the cleanup, this report is typically called a Corrective Action Plan (CAP). Regardless of the title, the Feasibility Study or Corrective Action Plan summarizes the findings of all prior reports and, most importantly, is intended to

- present a current evaluation of cleanup alternatives which are feasible at the site, and
- recommend a preferred cleanup alternative.

A site-specific cleanup alternative is selected by the consultant based upon the following factors:

60. See, 40 C.F.R. § 300.430(a)(2) (1995).

- The nature and extent of the contamination
- The site conditions
- Site limitations (near a river, close to the foundation of multi-story buildings; bordering a freeway or a school, etc.)
- Cost effectiveness of the various cleanup options
- The current or potential beneficial uses of the involved groundwater

In Los Angeles, the Los Angeles RWQCB requires several specific items in a Corrective Action Plan:

- Reviewing the site history, as well as the soil and groundwater analytical data
- Reviewing the regional hydrogeology and evaluating the site-specific hydrogeology
- Evaluating the water quality of nearby surface water or groundwater, and the current and potential beneficial uses
- Evaluating the nature of the contaminants, including the toxicity, persistence, and potential for migration in soil and groundwater
- Defining the extent of contamination in soil and groundwater
- Evaluating the treatability of the contaminants based on bench tests, pilot studies, or other literature and resources
- Defining the cleanup objectives of the correction action
- Identifying which technologies can achieve the objectives, based on the applicability, feasibility, reliability, and proven effectiveness of the technology when used at similar sites
- Evaluating the cleanup alternatives, including the "no action alternative," and at least two cleanup alternative methodologies which can treat the contamination at the site
- Recommending a cleanup alternative with justification
- Estimating the cost involved in construction, operation, maintenance, and decommissioning of the treatment system
- Developing a sampling and analysis plan to monitor cleanup progress, and to verify that the cleanup measures are effectively reducing contaminant concentrations
- Proposing cleanup levels acceptable to the Regional Board
- Identifying the regulatory agencies and any permits or variances

necessary to do the work
- Developing a time schedule for implementation
- Developing a health and safety plan

The Feasibility Study or Corrective Action Plan must be submitted to the appropriate regulatory agency with jurisdiction over the cleanup before any cleanup action is initiated.

In a CERCLA cleanup, upon completion of the Remedial Investigation / Feasibility Study (RI/FS) and remedy in process, the NCP requires that the analysis be reviewed by the US EPA. They must then issue a Record of Decision (ROD).[61] The ROD identifies the final selected remedy. A Remedial Action Plan ("RAP") will then be required to describe the design of the specific, chosen remedial action, including the operation, maintenance, and construction of the remedial action to take place.

RODs may also be interim. Here, again, you must be very careful. While a ROD must adhere to all state and federal environmental regulations, an interim ROD need not. It is important to note that in an interim ROD, while the federal government has signed on to a course of action, it is saying that it's not the permanent solution; otherwise, they would have issued a final ROD. An interim ROD exempts the federal authorities from complying with their own regulations. Again, be careful. Read the reports and all the underlying assumptions. They are not in fine print.

At some point in the future, the rules of engagement (read: war) will change. An interim ROD puts the project on roller skates. There is no definitive solution or course of action. The rules are in limbo, and so are the costs and a final remedy. The final chapter of an interim ROD, which would ordinarily describe a permanent cleanup solution, will state that a final clean up remedy has not yet been decided upon or funded. Expect projected future costs to rise. You can also assume that no one—the EPA, the state, or any fellow PRPs who are under the same orders you are—will be willing to completely let you off the hook until the final remedy has been chosen. In this regard, please note, it usually takes 30 years to implement the interim ROD. Therefore, no provision for the final remedy is typically made until approximately 30 years after the Superfund PRP has settled his purported liability for the interim remedy! It's a long process which can cover several lifetimes.

61. Acronyms for ROD and Responsiveness Survey at: http://www-erd.llnl.gov/library/rod/acronyms.html and http://www.em.doe.gov/cercla97/appenda.html.

6. Risk Assessment

A risk assessment is a report addressing whether the contamination present at the site constitutes a current or potential threat to human health and the environment. This report may be a subsection of a CERCLA Feasibility Study,[62] but is usually an entirely separate report that is used to determine whether the contamination present at the site constitutes a current or potential threat to human health and the environment. If the site contamination does pose a threat, this report will help to establish acceptable exposure levels for developing remedial alternatives.

The risk assessment typically describes the way contaminants at the site are

- migrating to groundwater or surface water,
- being released to the air—indoors or outside,
- leaching through the soil,
- remaining in the soil, or
- bioaccumulating in the food chain.

The risk assessment identifies the key contaminants and their relative toxicity. It also evaluates exposure pathways and risks to sensitive "receptors"—such as people living in nearby homes or in the location—and is described in detail in 40 C.F.R. § 300.430(d)(1) (1995).

Many consultants neither know how to use this report nor appreciate its incredible potential value in saving the client time and money. The concept of health risk assessment is most valuable in two situations. First, if the site is potentially within the jurisdiction of California's Department of Toxic Substances Control (DTSC), the DTSC has a site evaluation template which includes a procedure called a Preliminary Endangerment Assessment (PEA). It is a part of the DTSC's site mitigation process.

Once a site has been screened and identified as a known or potentially contaminated site, the PRP responsible for the site investigation may opt to perform a PEA. This report can help to determine "whether current or past waste management practices have resulted in the release or threatened release of hazardous substances which pose a threat to public

62. 40 C.F.R. § 300.430(d)(4).

health or the environment."[63] If the PRP— like you—completes a PEA according to the guidelines articulated by the DTSC's PEA Guidance Manual and recommends no further action, the DTSC can, upon review, release the site from any further action if it agrees with the PRP's recommendations.

Second, a valid risk assessment showing no potential harm to public health or the environment has another use. It may assist a PRP in obtaining closure for a site even when the cleanup goals or contamination levels promised by a Feasibility Study or Corrective Action Plan cannot be attained. The Regional Water Quality Control Board has recognized that it can be more expedient and appropriate to cease remediation based upon the results of a risk assessment. The Regional Board can determine, using a valid risk assessment / chemical transport model, whether the remaining contaminants left in place at a site pose a further unacceptable threat to the site occupants or a risk to site groundwater quality. If the risk assessment is valid, the Board could determine that future costs to further remediate the soil or groundwater would not be cost-effective or expedient based on the modeling data. If that is the case, the Regional Board may agree that no further action should be required.

Bottom line: If the risk of cancer from your site is calculated to result in less than one excess cancer death per one million people, you have a chance of closing the site without further remediation or cost.

63. Health & Saf. Code §25319.5.

Chapter IV: Do You Need an Environmental Consultant Before You File a Lawsuit or Before You Respond to a Lawsuit That's Been Filed Against You?

A. General Background

The answer to the question asked in this chapter title is a resounding "yes." An environmental consultant with interdisciplinary training in the major areas of technical expertise is invaluable. His or her analysis of soil and groundwater pollution cases is a critically important asset to the effective defense or prosecution of a pollution case. Your attorney's association with an environmental consultant who is aware of the synergies of environmental issues is really the only way to get a case on track quickly in its first stages.

Although the retention of the consultant may seem to be an unnecessary initial expense, in the long run, the use of an environmental "litigation consultant" may result in considerable savings. For instance, if your attorney associates with a competent environmental litigation consultant, this consultant can work with your attorney to choose the proper experts who will need to be designated for trial. Your attorney will be able to avoid over-designating in a scattershot manner. Counsel will also be able to choose the experts in question after short initial conferences instead of going through the time-consuming, costly, and iterative process of refining a list of likely experts, only to find that another expert is needed in a particular subject because the initial expert's experience or background does not fit the exact requirements of the attorney's case. The expert may have appeared to have the needed expertise on paper, but in fact may not be able to handle themselves effectively on the witness stand or in a deposition in front of opposing counsel.

The identities and opinions of experts retained by your attorney solely as consultants (to evaluate your case or to prepare for trial) are protected by the work-product privilege under California law[64] and under the Federal Rules of Civil Procedure.[65] Any reports prepared by the environmental litigation consultant to explain technical issues to the attorney—including diagrams and notes or memos—fall under the work-product doctrine.[66]

There are two issues to keep in mind when using an environmental litigation consultant in connection with asserting an entitlement to attorney work-product protection to shield the consultant's work and communications with the attorney who retains the consultant. First, while work-product protection is absolute where it concerns the attorney's impressions, conclusions, opinions, or legal research or theories,[67] it is only a "qualified" protection when it comes to consultants. Hypothetically, a court could order disclosure of the consultant's work product if denial of disclosure would unfairly prejudice the party seeking discovery or otherwise result in an injustice. For example, in the exceptional circumstance that the consultant is the only expert who is qualified on a particular subject, and no other experts are available on that subject, the court could order disclosure of the consultant's work-product.[68] In addition, where the consultant has performed testing or sampling which has been lost or is no longer available to the opposing party, that party could try to obtain discovery on that testing or sampling from the consultant.

It should also be noted that conversations or interviews that the environmental litigation consultant has with you, the client—to evaluate the prior uses of contaminated property or the possible presence or impact of hazardous substances on the property in question—would also be afforded absolute protection under the attorney-client privilege. As such, information disclosed to an agent of the attorney (i.e., the consultant) by the

64. Cal. Code Civ. Proc. § 2018(b).

65. Fed.R.Civ.P. 26(b)(4)(B).

66. *Williamson v. Superior Court (Shell Oil)* (1978) 21 Cal.3d 829, 834.

67. Cal. Code Civ. Proc. § 2018(c).

68. *Kenney v. Superior Court* (1967) 255 Cal.App.2d 106, 113; Weil & Brown, Cal. Prac. Guide: Civ. Pro. Before Trial, The Rutter Group (1996) § 8:248-8:250.

client for transmission to the attorney qualifies as an attorney-client communication.[69]

Second, you might consider having your attorney hire all consultants for you. That way, you'll have the possibility of having their work shielded under either the work-product privilege or the attorney-client privilege. This might be a good course of action even outside litigation, such as hiring a consultant to review environmental issues on land you currently own or land you intend to buy. If your consultant uncovers any negative information, you may want to avoid making it public before you have dealt with the issues or problems which were raised in the reports.

B. Technical Qualifications

To effectively advise you or your attorney in a soil and groundwater pollution case, the environmental litigation consultant must be knowledgeable in several environmental areas.

Civil Engineering

This branch of engineering is a great catchall for all things dealing with soil excavation, building construction, foundations for buildings, water supplies, canals, and so on. For a time, when the field of environmental engineering was young, many civil engineers became environmental engineers. Civil engineers can size water pipes, survey land, perform well borings, and do other such work. They often work with geologists. *Check the credentials of the civil engineer to confirm they also have environmental expertise and experience.* If they are a state-registered professional engineer, what is their specialty? Environmental agencies like the California Department of Toxic Substances Control (DTSC) require health risk assessments to be written as part of initial environmental evaluations. Many civil engineers either do not know the usefulness of health risk assessments, nor understand their true economic value in closing a site. If you ask them about health risk assessments, you may be very surprised by the answers you receive. Ask them if they have ever used a RBCA—risk-based closure assessment—to close a site. If they don't know what you are referring to, end the conversation and bid them a fond farewell. Civil engineers will be recognized by the State by being a PE—a state-registered professional engineer. This requires certified schooling, appropriate experience, and passing an eight-hour written test.

---

69. Evid. Code § 952.

Hydrogeology

These scientists specialize in water movement through the subsurface. They have a background in both geology and civil engineering (the latter to a lesser extent). They can plot groundwater movement through different types of geological formations and explain, or predict, how various chemicals move through the various soil environments.

Engineering Geology

While many geologists have been trained to view subsurface formations, and their specialty may encompass water flow, engineering geologists have their own state certification and regulatory board. They are concerned with engineered structures like dams, culverts, retaining walls, etc.

Environmental Toxicology

Public health issues are the litmus test in determining the severity of any type of contamination. The "public health and welfare" standard is an integral part of much federal and state environmental legislation. While toxicologists are not physicians, they are expert in assessing the impact of various chemicals—and to a lesser extent, drugs—on human body systems over various lengths of time. What an environmental engineer is to the environment, a toxicologist is to the human body. They are expert in writing and interpreting health risk assessments; that is, they can assess the assumed risk of cancer and other exposure-linked illnesses to various populations based on chemical stimuli coupled with specific site characteristics.

Real Estate Appraisal

Real estate appraisers can establish the current value of a property. They can determine what the sale price of a piece of property will be, given a willing buyer and seller and applying certain guidelines. Some appraisers have subspecialties that purport to determine the impact of "stigma" on a particular property, based upon both the contamination and the perceived reduction in value resulting from the general knowledge that the property has been contaminated, even if the contamination has been cleaned up.

General Contracting

General contractors construct buildings. They have a required, state-issued license which allows them to employ various specialty craftspeople like plumbers, electricians, and carpenters. There are no formal educational requirements to being a general contractor, though their work can be bonded.

Biostatistics

In the environmental context, a biostatistician has the expertise to review morbidity and cohort analyses to determine whether there is evidence of trends, correlations, or cause and effect relationships between human physiological problems (like cancer) and chemical agents or contaminants.

Environmental Contracting

Those who hold a general contractor's license may market themselves as environmental remediation contractors by paying an additional fee to the Contractors State License Board. The difference between a qualified environmental remediation contractor and an unqualified one lies in the contractor's knowledge of EPA treatment, storage, and disposal (TSD) regulations. Do they have an EPA transporter ID? If they do not know what you are talking about, keep looking.

Geology

These rockhounds see beauty in dirt, rocks, and water. Geologists can tell you whether your site will retain water, or if it has subterranean sources of water, perched water tables, clay lenses, or a subsurface soil stratigraphy (structure) that will allow transport of contamination within your site or permit offsite migration. Geologists can describe the history of your site going back millions of years. They can calculate the direction and speed of groundwater and explain acronyms like DNAPL (dense non-aqueous phase liquids)[70] and terms like "adsorption." They can also assess the ability of the site soils to permit liquids

---

70. Many organic solvents are denser than water, hence the designation "dense." DNAPLs sink through the water column and collect in depressions at the base of the water table. They flow along the bottom of the water table aquifer and can move in directions that are different than groundwater flow. DNAPL sources are difficult to locate and remediate, primarily for these reasons.

and groundwater to flow through them. They can determine if there are any subsurface structures or geological formations that would act as barriers to the flow of groundwater, either horizontally or vertically, through the soil column.

CASE STUDY 7: What's Groundwater Got to Do with It?

The lawyer co-author of this book was once asked to help a new client in litigation. The basis for the litigation was that hazardous chemical contamination on the client's property was believed to be migrating through the soil, entering groundwater and migrating into the soil and groundwater in the vicinity of the plaintiff's property, which was located immediately adjacent to the client's property. The lawyer asked his environmental consultant co-author to review the environmental data on the defendant's site. The data consisted of a substantial file of groundwater and soil data tables, maps, and environmental reports, written by three different environmental consulting firms over a ten-year period. This litigation had been going on for a while. Each law firm–there had been three–had commissioned an environmental report, and each law firm had a different environmental consultant. We agreed that it would be useful to review all of the existing technical documentation. Both lawyer and client authorized the review, which took about a month.

After having reviewed the documentation, the consultant walked into the lawyer's office to announce his conclusion: if you read all the documentation together–not sequentially–it demonstrated the exact opposite of what had been alleged. The polluting activities on the adjoining parcel had damaged the client's property–not the other way around, as had been alleged in the litigation for years. The documentation described a groundwater flow direction toward the client's property–not the other way around! The client was the damaged party, not the plaintiff, and it was the client who was justified in seeking damages. The lawyer, surprised but also somewhat relieved, promptly filed a motion for summary judgment (or "MSJ").

Apparently, the plaintiff had filed similar lawsuits against other defendants, with similar accusations of causing migration of contamination onto plaintiff's parcel. The plaintiff clearly did not want the summary judgement motion to be heard or for an adverse MSJ ruling to be in the record. The plaintiff dismissed the lawsuit against our client with prejudice.

Spectacular, huh? It's amazing what can happen if you look at the data!

Chemistry

Some chemical pollutants are problems just by themselves. Others cause problems due to their exposure to, or interaction with, other chemicals, or due to the addition of heat, cold, electricity, or time. Knowledge of these potential interactions is no small matter when it comes to assessing the impact of a chemical spill on a plot of land or to groundwater. The issues raised by chemical interactions play out on a human scale, where toxicologists or hydrologists may be needed. Understanding chemical interactions is very complex. The ability to analyze the continuing migration and appropriate cleanup of chemicals requires knowledge gleaned from many disciplines. Central to any evaluation is the knowledge of how the chemicals interact with each other and of their subsequent impact on the environment and human health.

Boots on the Ground: Are Environmental Investigations Privileged?[71]

There are exceptions to every rule. We are constantly presented with the following fact pattern queries from fellow lawyers and consultants, but most of all from either current or prospective clients: "I want you to retain Super Great Consulting to perform a site investigation at my precious parcel and prepare a confidential report. The great thing about this is that if I hire you and you hire our environmental consultant, and if we don't like what we find (if the site is screaming hot with contamination caused by my prior tenants, who manufactured computer circuit boards there for 30 years), we can bury the data through the attorney-client and attorney work-product privileges—right?"

Wrong! Unfortunately.

Please review California Health & Safety Code Section 25359.4. On the surface, it would appear that only owners or operators would have a duty to report a release of a "reportable quantity" of a hazardous substance into the environment, as the penalty provision of the statute provides that the owner of a property on which a reportable release has occurred, and any person who releases or causes a reportable release, shall be liable for a penalty of $25,000 for each violation and for each day that a violation continues if

71. This cautionary tale appeared as an article by the authors of this book in the July 13, 2022 issue of the *Los Angeles Daily Journal*.

they fail to submit a written report to the California Department of Toxic Substances Control ("DTSC") within 30 days of discovery of the release.

However, the reporting obligation is a broad one. It covers all sales, leases, and rentals of contaminated property once the contamination is discovered. Please also review California Health & Safety Code Section 25359.7. This section provides, in pertinent part:

> (a) Any owner of nonresidential real property who knows, or has reasonable cause to believe, that any release of hazardous substance has come to be located on or beneath that real property shall, prior to the sale, lease, or rental of the real property by that owner, give written notice of that condition to the buyer, lessee, or renter of the real property.

Section 25359.7 of the California Health & Safety Code applies equally to tenants, such that

> any lessee or renter of real property who knows or has reasonable cause to believe that any release of a hazardous substance has come or will come to be located on or beneath that real property shall, within a reasonable period of time . . . following the discovery by the lessee or renter of the presence or believed presence of the hazardous substance release, give written notice

of that condition to the owner of the real property or to the lessor under the lessee's or renter's lease or rental agreement.

What is a "reportable quantity" as the term is referenced in Section 25359.4? It's either the quantity of a hazardous substance established in Part 302 of Title 40 of the Code of Federal Regulations, or "any quantity of a hazardous substance that is not reportable "but that may pose a significant threat to public health and safety or to the environment."

Obviously, this is very broad. And you may have questions. If so, refer to DTSC's Fact Sheet Update, January 2008, entitled "Reporting Nonemergency Hazardous Substances Releases"—including the guidance section, "Commonly Asked Questions." There you will learn that if you receive a report which indicates that groundwater is contaminated with hazardous substances which may have been released at the site due to operations previously conducted at a facility there, a "written report is required within 30 days of discovery because groundwater has been impacted."

The DTSC Fact Sheet provides several pertinent scenarios for you to consider. It's important to review these scenarios and then talk with someone more knowledgeable than yourself to clarify your legal position.

In the DTSC Fact Sheet, you will also learn it is DTSC's position that "consulting firms are required to report nonemergency releases." As such, if the client has a duty to report, the client's consultant usually does also. You may get some blowback—but remember who is writing the checks. This might be a good time to review their insurance policies for errors and omissions, if they have them.

A colleague—James C. Macdonald, Esq. (jcm@jcmacdonald.com)—has helpfully pointed out at least one potential loophole. A prospective purchaser, pursuant to a purchase agreement, could agree to withhold the results of any investigation to the seller or any regulatory agency as part of the contract to allow an investigation to occur to see whether the buyer wants to move forward with the purchase. In that instance, the buyer's consultant would have the same reporting duties as the party retaining the consultant. Since the buyer won't have any reporting duties, neither will the buyer's consultant, and if the buyer retains the consultant, no reporting duty will exist if the results are not disclosed to the seller.

One rule of thumb: If the area of the *incident's* geographic footprint you are concerned with has already been reported to the California Office of Emergency Services (OES) or the local emergency response agencies, you are *probably* not required to report the property again. But each situation is different—there is no blanket amnesty from regulatory reporting requirements. Keep in mind that the operative issue is protection of the public health and safety from unknown contaminant exposure—not protection of your pocketbook, or your client's. There is clearly a higher standard.

When in doubt, report the incident—it's defensible. There is no penalty for reporting twice.

C. Specific Uses of the Environmental Litigation Consultant in the First Thirty Days

1. Initial Client Interview and First Site Visit

If the initial interview with your attorney and first site visit can take place simultaneously, two of the most important initial steps can be taken at the same time. To get a preliminary feel for the environmental issues affecting your situation, it is critical that your attorney and the consultant see the contaminated property. This seems ludicrous to emphasize, but many attorneys and consultants get so quickly overwhelmed with the minutiae in environmental disputes that they forget to take some of the foundational steps necessary to understand the critical issues in the case. You need to "kick dirt."

It can be tremendously helpful to have the environmental consultant present when your attorney initially interviews you. This way, the consultant can identify related issues concerning past use of the property and industry-specific issues associated with hazardous substances that may not be readily apparent. The environmental litigation consultant will have a different take on the data. You can save a lot of time by having the consultant participate in the initial client interview.

VERY IMPORTANT: Although you may have several site assessment reports to turn over to your counsel and your environmental litigation consultant, looking at report maps only has meaning if the individuals studying the map have actually "kicked dirt" and roamed the property to get an in-person sense of the physical location.

2. Public Records Requests

There is a tangled and overlapping web of public regulatory agencies that may have jurisdiction over the contamination at issue. Some party involved in the polluted property may have (historically) reported a release or spill to any one of several potential agencies. First, it is critically important to identify all public regulatory agencies that have had anything to do with the contaminated property in question. Second, one of the most important issues that may arise is which public regulatory agency has primary jurisdiction or has been identified as the lead agency over the site investigation at issue. This is particularly relevant if you are sued by a private party while you are performing or operating under a cleanup and abatement order (CAO) from a state or federal regulatory agency. If this is the case, a legal principle called the "primary jurisdiction doctrine" may apply, and you may be able to stay (i.e., to put a "freeze" on) the action against you until you have completed your work under the governmental order. By that time, the sting will have been taken off your dispute, and the purported damages will be lessened or at least quantified.

Every potential regulatory agency is important. Public records inquiries and formal requests, if necessary, should be made to all agencies, including the local and county fire departments, Air Quality Management District (AQMD), the city or county Department of Public Works (DPW), the Regional Water Quality Control Board (RWQCB), California Department of Toxic Substances Control (DTSC), and the United States Environmental Protection Agency (EPA)—each of which may have jurisdiction over the site and be the primary repository of public records documents which you will need to review.

Public records requests to the EPA are made pursuant to the Freedom of Information Act (FOIA) 5 U.S.C. § 552. Public records requests to State agencies are made pursuant to the California Public Records Act, Government Code §§ 6250.

Your attorney should be careful to obtain certified copies of the records if you need to use any notes, memoranda, or reports in the public entity's file as evidence in the case. Certified copies bear some extra marker of authenticity, such as a stamp or attached declaration signed by an authorized agent of the organization. Some agencies have "custodian of records" forms that they provide to establish a foundation of authenticity. Other agencies may ask the attorney to prepare a declaration or affidavit for the agency's custodian of records to execute. Dealing with this little headache at the onset of the case (or before it) is far preferable to scrambling at the time of a trial to get the evidence in line when opposing counsel is no longer willing to enter into any stipulations concerning authenticity.

3. Initial Technical Analysis

Your attorney and the environmental litigation consultant should separately review all the site investigation reports and technical data obtained from you and the relevant regulatory agencies. After their initial review, the attorney and consultant should compare notes. At this point, important decisions will be made which will create the road map for the journey toward or away from early resolution.

If your liability is clear, and there is an existing lawsuit, but plaintiff and other defendants already named in the suit are also clearly liable, your attorney may want to propose a *tolling agreement* or temporary stay (i.e., "freeze") on litigation activities among all parties. This agreement or stipulation may set the stage for an allocation or apportionment of liability to be negotiated between all parties. On the other hand, the initial technical analysis may reveal that not all the contributors to the contamination have been named as parties. There may be other potentially responsible parties (PRPs) who should be identified and further investigated to determine whether they should be notified or pursued in litigation.

In addition, performing an initial review of all available technical data—if substantial studies have been performed and/or any cleanup work has been conducted—may enable the environmental litigation consultant to recommend whether an action should be filed against any environmental consultants who previously performed work on the property. At this stage, a cross-check should be made to ensure that all your employees or contractors (who may have been involved with the polluting events or may know of activities which resulted in the pollution) have been interviewed.

If your property is a site that has arranged for the disposal of hazardous waste at a landfill, you should determine whether you have copies of your hauling records, federal waste manifests, and disposal invoices. If you have requested copies from any regulatory agencies, those copies can be cross-checked against your records for accuracy. Discrepancies can occur because sometimes your waste volume may have been combined with other wastes picked up by the transporter or disposal company en route to the dump. In this case the EPA may have recorded the total volume from the transporter, rather than the volume of your individual load. In other instances, if the writing on the manifest is unclear, the EPA sometimes picks the largest possible volume which you ever disposed of and attributes that value to the illegible manifest (an illogical default strategy). Sometimes a clerical error results in misreading the manifests or computational errors. It's a dull but worthy task to review the manifests and cross-check them with other invoices and tallies. We have saved clients thousands of dollars by doing this sort of slow, precise "bean counting." We have reviewed our findings with the client, who often has a pretty good sense of how much hazardous waste they disposed of over the years.

In addition, if it appears that the contamination at issue preceded your purchase or lease of the property, the environmental litigation consultant should perform, if possible, an age-dating Carbon-14 analysis of the chemical contaminants of concern. This can determine the dates of the contamination, within certain limits.[72] Note that age-dating will not work to establish earliest dates of use of PCE, TCE, or vinyl chloride.

4. Assistance with Insurance Claims

It is imperative that you tender the third-party liability claim to your liability insurance carrier as soon as possible after service of the suit against you has been received. Otherwise, if the insurer accepts the defense and agrees to provide the defense under a "reservation of rights,"[73] it may refuse to reimburse the insured—that's you—for defense fees and costs incurred prior to the date it received formal notice of the claim. Fees incurred prior to formal notice are commonly called "pre-tender fees."

If you're the one filing suit, don't be surprised if you get sued back, and don't forget to tender or submit the countersuit to your insurers, or to the insurers of your lessees or subcontractors (if they've listed you as an additional insured by way of endorsement on their liability insurance policies). Although no one likes to be sued (and it certainly does not provide a warm and cozy "Hallmark card" feeling), this can be one of the best ways to put together a communal settlement pot to resolve a case in the early stages.

Let's say that of the twenty years you have owned the property, you operated an auto body shop there for five years, and your tenant bought the business from you and has run it on the site for the last fifteen years. Assume that there is insurance (as explained in

72. Radiocarbon dating is a method that provides age estimates for carbon-based materials that originated from living organisms. Plants and animals assimilate carbon 14 from carbon dioxide throughout their lifetimes. When they die, they stop exchanging carbon with the biosphere and their carbon 14 content then starts to decrease at a rate determined by the law of radioactive decay. Radiocarbon dating is essentially a method designed to measure residual radioactivity.

73. A "reservation of rights" is a letter from the insurer to its insured, which is transmitted after the insurer has determined that a potential for coverage exists under the policy and there is a duty to defend. A proper reservation of rights letter will set forth the key terms, conditions and limitations of the applicable policies and will also set forth the salient facts at issue in the claim which both trigger the defense obligation and also limit that obligation. The purpose of the reservation of rights letter is to protect the insurer's right to withdraw from the defense if further facts are developed which eliminate the potential for coverage. In addition, the insurer may reserve its right to seek reimbursement of fees paid for the defense if it turns out there is no coverage. The insurer may also reserve its right to seek reimbursement of defense fees paid if further investigation of facts developed in the underlying action show that there is no potential for indemnity, such as if the alleged property damage does not constitute an "occurrence" under the policy or if the property damage falls within the policy's exclusions. In this regard, the insurer might reserve its right to decline to indemnify its insured against a non-covered judgment or settlement rendered in the action.

greater detail below), and also assume that a dispute exists as to when the contamination occurred during the twenty-year period. If you're an additional insured on your tenant's policy, when the insurer for your tenant settles the tenant's liability, if the tenant has filed a cross-complaint or counterclaim against you for contribution or indemnity for the five-year period you allegedly polluted the property, the same insurer will most likely pay a percentage of the cleanup costs to the tenant rather than incur substantial defense costs and attorneys' fees trying to prove that the contamination did not occur during the five years you operated the business. If the tenant agrees to assign his recovery to you for the sole purpose of cleaning up the property, the total cost of the cleanup will have been funded by insurance, with no out-of-pocket cost to either tenant or landlord.

But we are getting a little ahead of ourselves here. There are other nuances in the world of insurance that you should understand.

Typically, after receiving notice of a claim, the liability insurer will begin its coverage investigation. They will usually require the assistance of coverage counsel (retained by the insurer) because of the high potential for litigation expenses and substantial financial risk inherent in environmental litigation.

Comprehensive general liability policies (CGL) obligate the liability insurer to defend its insured against any suit alleging covered bodily injury or property damage that raises a "potential for indemnity" under the policy.[74]

For years, policy holder attorneys argued that the concept of the term "suit" as used in CGL policies could have other meanings, in addition to simply referring to formal lawsuits filed in a court of law. It has been argued that a "suit" also encompasses state or federal administrative proceedings, or orders which could be construed as the functional equivalent of a suit, triggering the insurer's duty to defend even before a formal lawsuit is filed against the insured. The rationale for this "functional" (as opposed to "literal") approach is that the term "suit" is not defined in most CGL policies. Therefore, it should be subject to a more expansive interpretation in favor of the insured's objectively reasonable expectations. Because the amount of the insured's damage liability or cleanup responsibility may be determined through Cal-EPA or EPA proceedings or orders, these governmental demands, which are adversarial or coercive in nature, are arguably more than a mere "claim" because of their potential preclusive effect of fixing or determining liability and damages in a pre-lawsuit proceeding.

The "claim versus suit" issue has been resolved by the California Supreme Court

---

74. *Montrose Chemical Corp. v. Admiral Ins. Co.* (1995) 10 Cal.4th 645, 659 fn. 9 (*Montrose II*); *Vann v. Travelers Companies* (1995) 39 Cal.App.4th 1610, 1614.

as to the duty to defend (i.e., the duty to pay for a lawyer to defend you) and the duty to indemnify (i.e., the duty to fund a settlement or pay a judgment against you and/or to pay for cleanup costs). The court adopted the "literal" meaning approach advocated by insurance companies for the interpretation of the meaning of "suit." Thus, as the law stands presently, a liability insurer has a duty to defend or indemnify only a suit filed against an insured in a court of law.[75] This means that if you have received

- a PRP notice from the EPA under CERCLA;
- a cleanup and abatement order from one of the California Regional Water Quality Control Boards; or
- an imminent and substantial endangerment order from DTSC,

your liability insurer will have no obligation to reimburse you for your legal fees or to furnish you with insurer-appointed counsel if the policy provides only for a defense against a "suit."

The reason? No lawsuit has been filed against you in a court of law. Almost all administrative proceedings, no matter how threatening or coercive in terms of monetary demands or threatened penalties, are only "claims" or "demands" which an insurer has no duty to defend and no duty to pay for in any way under California law.[76]

This means if you haven't been sued by anybody, you're up the proverbial creek, as far as finding any potential coverage under old liability insurance policies goes. It would still be wise to check with an environmental insurance coverage lawyer if you receive an administrative request or order from a federal or state environmental regulatory agency—as certain exceptions may apply. In particular, the insurer's duty to settle claims, a separate and independent duty, may require the insurer to settle where the insured's liability is a foregone conclusion. In addition, please note that the California rule on the duty to defend and indemnify governmental claims represents a minority view on the issue among jurisdictions which have considered environmental coverage disputes. Finally, there may be a choice of law question if the insured lives in California, but the property is located out

---

75. *Foster-Gardner, Inc. v. National Union Fire Ins. Co.* (1998) 18 Cal.4th 857, 878-879 (defense duty); *Certain Underwriters At Lloyd's, London v. Superior Court (Powerine Oil Co.)* (1999) 24 Cal.4th 945 (duty to indemnify).

76. We hesitate to state the proposition in an absolute sense, as the California Supreme Court recently held that administrative adjudicative proceedings before an administrative law judge, which involved twenty-two days of trial, numerous witnesses, and substantial evidence, constituted a "suit" triggering an insurer's duty to defend. See *Ameron International Corporation v. Insurance Co.* (2010) 50 Cal.4th 1370, 1374.

of state—this could provide for a more favorable rule of insurance coverage.

One exception occurs in older policies with "claim or suit" language, like so: "The Company shall have the right and duty to defend any *claim or suit* against the insured seeking damages payable under this policy." If the policy provides coverage for "any claim or suit," the claim will most likely be accepted by the insurer, at least for defense purposes.

The following analysis applies in situations where you have been sued. Although almost all CGL policies issued after 1986 contain what is called an "absolute pollution exclusion, policies issued between 1973 (or slightly before) and 1986 commonly contain a "sudden and accidental" pollution exclusion. If you are lucky enough to locate a general liability policy issued prior to 1970 (or shortly thereafter), it is unlikely that the policy will even contain a pollution exclusion clause.

The "sudden and accidental" pollution exclusion states that the insurance does not apply to property damage

> arising out of the discharge, dispersal, release or escape of toxic chemicals, liquid or gasses, waste materials or other irritants, contaminants or pollutants into or upon land, the atmosphere or any water course or body of water; but this exclusion does not apply if such discharge, dispersal, release or escape is sudden and accidental . . .

The 1973 to 1985 CGL policy forms (and most pre-1973 and post-1985 policy forms) also contain an "owned property" exclusion which provides:

> "This insurance does not apply:
> 1. to property damage to
> 2. property owned or occupied by or rented to the insured;
> 3. property used by the insured; or
> 4. property in the care, custody, or control of the insured or as to which the insured is for any purpose exercising physical control . . .

Liability policies are usually occurrence-based. The term "occurrence" is typically defined as "an accident, including injurious exposure to conditions, which results, during the policy period, in bodily injury or property damage neither expected nor intended from the standpoint of the insured."

Although there are at least four different insurance coverage theories for trigger of coverage[77] (exposure, injury-in-fact, manifestation, and continuing injury), the only theory of importance in California is a continuing (or multiple) trigger approach which has been adopted by the California Supreme Court. In the case of successive policies, the California Supreme Court has ruled that "bodily injury and property damage that is continuous or progressively deteriorating throughout several policy periods is potentially covered by all policies in effect during those periods."[78] Thus, in California, the "continuous injury" trigger of coverage has been adopted for third-party liability insurance cases involving continuous or progressively deteriorating losses.[79]

Consequently, if there is any real (i.e., non-conjectural) possibility that the property damage alleged against the client occurred during the policy period, the insurance carrier's defense obligation should be triggered[80] unless the insurer can conclusively demonstrate—using undisputed facts obtained from the complaint, the insured, or extraneous sources—that there is no "potential for coverage."[81] The liability insurer's investigation will attempt to determine whether the contamination is limited to the insured's own property (and coverage is therefore barred by the "owned property" exclusion)—or whether the contamination has taken place gradually over an extended period of time such that there is no possibility that the "sudden and accidental" exception to the pollution exclusion would apply.[82]

---

77. In the third-party liability insurance context, the term "trigger of coverage" denotes "the circumstances that activate the insurer's defense and indemnity obligations under the policy... [T]rigger of coverage is a term of convenience used to describe that which, under the specific terms of an insurance policy, must happen in the policy period in order for the potential of coverage to arise. The issue is largely one of timing what must take place within the policy's effective dates for the potential of coverage to be 'triggered.'" *Montrose II*, supra, 10 Cal.4th at 655, fn. 2.

78. Id. at 655.

79. Ibid.

80. In this regard, the timing of the accident, event or conditions causing the property damage can occur before or during the policy period. "It is only the effect of the occurrence of bodily injury or property damage during the policy period, resulting from a sudden accidental event or the 'continuous or repeated exposure to conditions' that triggers potential liability coverage." *Montrose II* at 675.

81. *Vann v. Travelers Companies*, supra, 3 Cal.App.4th at 1615.

82. See, *Shell Oil Co. v. Winterthur Swiss Ins. Co.* (1993) 12 Cal.App.4th 715, 752-56; *ACL Technologies, Inc. v. Northbrook Property & Casualty Ins. Co.* (1993) 17 Cal.App.4th 1773, 1787; *Smith v. Hughes Aircraft Co.*, 22 F.3d 1432 (9th Cir. 1993).

CASE STUDY 8:
On the Waterfront

In a famous scene from the seminal motion picture *On the Waterfront*, Terry Malloy (Marlon Brando) says to his brother Charley (Rod Steiger), "I coulda had class. I coulda been a contender. I coulda been somebody, instead of a bum, which is what I am, let's face it." We have heard similar laments from our clients over the years as they crumble under the threats of sanctions from the EPA, an attorney general threatening an enforcement action, or just the garden-variety private litigant who has sued the client for every penny.

We're exaggerating slightly, but the overall point remains: most clients want to give up before they even try. The first thing we ask is whether they had comprehensive general liability (CGL) insurance going back to the beginning of time with their property or business. Sadly, they usually say they purged their old files. What use could a 40-year-old insurance policy possibly have?

As we discuss in this text, liability insurance is occurrence-based, meaning that if the property damage was continuous, with no clear starting or ending point, all liability coverage is triggered over the years unless the loss is otherwise excluded by the policy language.

Even if the policies have been lost or destroyed, there may be other indicia or secondary evidence which can prove that coverage was in place many years ago. For example, we had a fantastic client many years ago whose company had been notified of its potential liability at a major Superfund site in the San Fernando Valley. The EPA and the PRP (potentially responsible party) group were extremely aggressive. The client had just sold his business to a large company but retained the liability. He was all set for retirement but would never be able to enjoy it if he had to continue defending against the claims of the EPA and the PRP group. He was going down. He was desperate as he sadly recalled the glory days of his business, and what a tight ship he thought he had run when it came to handling hazardous substances and hazardous waste.

We pushed the client to go back to his storage facility one more time and look through every scrap of paper in his old files. He didn't find the actual insurance policies, but he did find a few letters–one from a major insurer and the other from the insurance defense lawyer retained by the insurer to defend the company in an employment suit more than 20 years earlier. It was a tangled web, but it led to the discovery of more than $1 million in liability coverage in multiple insurance policies, which did not exclude property damage caused by environmental contamination.

Bingo! After fighting the insurance company for a while, our client was able to pay off his mortgage and go fly fishing at a fabulous resort (we know it was spectacular, because we went there ourselves on his recommendation). Case closed.

The owned property exclusion is usually a relatively easy hurdle to surmount, due to the fact that groundwater contamination is typically alleged in most pollution cases, and California courts have routinely held that groundwater belongs to the state of California (i.e., a third party) and not to the insured.[83] Further, even if groundwater contamination is not present, there is often an imminent threat of groundwater contamination which also

83. *Titan Corp. v. Aetna Casualty & Surety Co.* (1994) 22 Cal.App.4th 457, 471-472.

nullifies the application of this particular exclusion.[84] In addition, if the soil contamination plume has spread (or is threatening to spread) beyond the insured's property to adjacent neighboring properties, the "owned property" exclusion would also be negated.

Despite the broad duty to defend recognized by California courts, several Ninth Circuit and California appellate courts have recently held that the "sudden and accidental" exception to the pollution exclusion is akin to the coverage grant language of a CGL policy. Just as the burden of showing the potential of an "occurrence" during the policy period is on the insured, the insured must therefore also carry the burden of showing that the property damage at issue was caused by a "sudden and accidental" discharge or release to be entitled to coverage.[85] Note that these cases apply only to the duty to indemnify, not the duty to defend.

Where information is sought by the insurer concerning the purported absence of offsite soil or groundwater contaminant migration (which puts the "owned property" exclusion in play), the environmental litigation consultant may be able to easily resolve the issue in the insured's favor by assembling critical sampling data to demonstrate the presence or threat of offsite soil or groundwater contamination. Crucially, in examining the application of the pollution exclusion, even where historic sudden and accidental discharges or releases may have escaped notice, and record keeping may have been lost or buried with ex-employees or deceased former owners and operators, there are still options. The environmental litigation consultant may be able to resurrect these ancient events for the purpose of showing that the site contamination potentially or actually resulted from sudden and accidental spills.

For example, if one spills or otherwise releases a chlorinated solvent like PCE on the surface of the ground or onto concrete, the liquid will be absorbed into the ground (through the concrete) at a rate which is governed by the type of soil (compacted, clay, loose gravel, silty, etc.). The movement of the liquid through the soil will also be governed by additional factors such as the viscosity of the liquid: thick and high viscosity, like molasses; or perhaps thin and low viscosity, like water. Chlorinated solvents have more of the characteristics of water than most waste oils, which are like molasses. If solvents are released into the soil gradually over time, one would expect a larger concentration of the liquid would be near the surface and over time would gradually seep through the soil.

---

84. Ibid.

85. See, *Aeroquip Corp. v. Aetna Casualty & Surety Co., Inc.*, 26 F.3d 893, 894-95 (9th Cir. 1994); *Haskel, Inc. v. Superior Court* (1995) 33 Cal.App.4th 963, 977, fn. 13; *Aydin Corp v. First State Ins. Co.* (1998) 18 Cal.4th 1183, 1194.

To understand how the concentrations of solvents move through soil over time, one can think of a "pyramid" shape. Looking at the soil beneath the surface, the "top" of the pyramid, or area closest to the surface, would likely have the highest solvent concentration. Progressively deeper tests of soils, toward the "base" of the pyramid, would reveal a gradual, decreasing solvent concentration in the soil. In other words, if there were a gradual solvent release over time, one would expect the soils close to the surface of the ground to reflect a higher concentration of the solvents, which would then slowly decrease in concentration the deeper in the ground subsequent soil tests were performed. Therefore, a characteristic of a gradual solvent release would be a high solvent concentration near the surface and slowly decreasing solvent concentration in the soil, the deeper one tested.

On the other hand, an historically discrete spill event (such as the rupture of an above-ground or underground chemical storage tank) would result in soil solvent concentrations progressively decreasing in soil depth, until observation of a sudden increase in concentration at depth becomes evident. This higher subsurface solvent concentration reflects the existence of an historic spill: one that had preceded the release confirmed from the decreasing solvent data, physically above this increased concentration datum point in the soil and closer to the surface. It is as though this point of higher concentration was at the surface earlier but has moved down through the soil over time.

Therefore, instances where the same chemicals have measured concentrations which decrease with depth over time, then are measured at high concentrations at still lower depths, indicate historic sudden and accidental events on the surface. If the introduction of these solvents were made gradually into the soil over time, the chemical concentration data would never exhibit a sudden increase in the concentration in the soil as the distance from the surface increased downward.

Thus, when the consultant examines soil sampling data, they may be able to pinpoint certain specific site areas (e.g., vapor degreasers used for parts cleaning or metal plating and hazardous materials storage areas) where significant sudden and accidental spills have occurred. If the consultant shares this information with the lawyer in a written memo (to preserve the work-product privilege), and the lawyer then forwards the information to the insurer, the result can be the offer of a defense which otherwise might not have materialized. The consultant's use of simple illustrated tables and figures can also assist in making an effective presentation.

Chapter V:

Unusual Party Guests

Throughout this practice guide, we have referenced the usual defendants or responsible parties: the property owner, the property operator or lessee, or the hazardous waste generator who arranges for the disposal of spent materials at a landfill. In addition, we have mentioned the unfortunate circumstance in which an environmental consultant hired to address a cleanup can be legally responsible for either ignoring a problem, or for an "overkill" approach to eradicate alleged contamination that either doesn't have to be remediated to the level chosen or that doesn't even require cleanup at all.

Here are two other types of potential defendants or co-responsible parties to consider.

A. Dead People[86]

Imagine that you once ran a small metal plating business, called Joe's Plating, at a site that you leased and occupied for five years. You acquired the business from Joe Nomore who had started Joe's Plating at this location and ran it there for approximately ten years. You leased and occupied the site in question for only five years before selling the business to the current operator. Joe Nomore has since died. The owner of the property recently

86. This section, in slightly altered form, appeared originally in the Advisor (Environmental Law) section of the *Los Angeles Daily Journal*, March 29, 1999, as "Insurance Policy May Allow One to Raise the Dead," by co-author Murray Sinclair.

discovered extensive soil and groundwater contamination in the course of performing a Phase II environmental investigation to refinance the property. That owner is now suing you and the current operator.

You may feel inclined to ask: if federal and state environmental statutes and garden-variety state law nuisance claims all operate on a strict liability theory, then why should Joe Nomore (who has not been named in the action and is deceased) not be held accountable for his actions during the ten-year period he ran the business—especially considering that significant solvent spills took place at the facility during the period of his tenancy?

This is a good question. Joe's Plating was a sole proprietorship, not a corporation, so at first glance it may seem like there is not much that can be done. Joe died years ago. The probate on his estate has long since closed. Therefore, unlike a dissolved corporation which may maintain a registered agent for service of process, or which might have former officers and directors who can also be served, there is no one but Joe's ghost upon whom to serve a third-party contribution complaint or cross-complaint.

Are you sunk? Yes and no. If the comprehensive general liability policies that Joe maintained on the business have been lost, there is nothing you can do. However—if any of Joe's policies can be found, the late Joe is still potentially very much "alive" as a potential contribution source.

Similar to pursuing actions against dissolved corporations, if an individual decedent had liability insurance, an action may be maintained against the decedent's estate pursuant to sections 550 through 555 of the California Probate Code, with service upon an agent of the insurer.[87] The principle is obvious, although it appears to be little used in most litigation. When the probate code was revised in 1987, the California Law Revision Commission acknowledged that, of the many statutes governing litigation against a decedent, "among the most complex and confusing are those relating to claims covered by insurance."[88] As such, the code was simplified to allow a creditor to proceed directly against the insurer for recovery, instead of through the estate or against successors-in-interest.

The statute of limitations of Probate Code Section 551 will rarely act as a bar to a third party complaint or cross-complaint because of the delayed discovery rule, which operates in most environmental cases to toll the statute of limitations until the plaintiff knows, or should reasonably suspect, injury or damage has occurred.[89] Under Section 551,

---

87. See *Penasquitos, Inc. v. Superior Court* (1991) 53 Cal.3d 1180, 1184.

88. Recommendation Relating to Litigation Involving Decedents, 19 Cal. L. Revision Comm'n Reports 899, 904 (1988).

89. See *Romo v. Estate of Bennett* (1979) 97 Cal.App.3d 304 (allowing suit under prior statute where

if the limitations period has not expired at the time of the decedent's death, an action under the Probate Code "may be commenced within one year after the expiration of the limitations period otherwise applicable."

The procedure is simple. The defendant must be named as "Estate of Joe Nomore, Deceased." Summons is then served on the insurers that issued any liability policies to Joe. When the summons and complaint are prepared, care should be taken to emphasize that the insurer is being sued in the capacity of designee or agent of the insured, and that it is not the insurer itself that is being sued (as in a bad-faith action). Under Probate Code Section 553, the insurer who is sued may deny or contest its liability. Further, unless the personal representative of the decedent is joined as a party to the action, any recovery will be confined to the "limits and coverage of the insurance" available.[90] Finally, it should be noted that a separate action to enforce any judgment obtained under Insurance Code Section 11580 is not necessary if the action against the insurer is brought under the probate code. Section 554 allows enforcement against the insurer by writ of execution.

This method of pursuing liability against a decedent's insurance assets benefits both the insured and the insurer. The more orphan shares of liability that must be distributed between the parties (i.e., shares of liability attributable to insolvent entities or deceased individuals with no funding capacity), the greater all parties' proportionate liability. In this regard, where orphan shares exist, the cost of orphan shares will be distributed among all the parties with funding capacity in addition to the amount they otherwise would have paid.[91]

This method of proceeding under the probate code allows for a more equitable and lower apportionment if you can succeed in establishing the decedent's covered liability under the policies that have been located. If an insurance carrier is providing for your defense, the claims representative should be pleased to know the carrier will be saving money by allocating the risk over a greater number of policies (unless, of course, the same carrier also insured the decedent).

Your attorney's first obligation is to attempt to fully protect the interests of his client. Using the probate code as a vehicle to obtain access to more coverage to indemnify a loss than would otherwise be available serves that worthy goal.

---

decedent's medical malpractice not discovered until nine years after decedent's death).

90. Prob. Code § 554.

91. *Pinal Creek Group v. Newmont Mining Corp.* (9th Cir. 1997) 118 F.3d 1298.

B. Potential Municipality Defendants

State and local governmental agencies which operate landfills and sewer systems—agencies also known as publicly owned treatment works (POTW)—may be liable under CERCLA or state law theories. In a typical dry cleaner's private party CERCLA cost recovery action, in which a dry cleaning solvent (PCE or TCE) release has occurred, the current owner of a shopping center will bring a cost recovery action against 1) all prior owners of the shopping center and 2) prior and current operators of the dry cleaning plant.

Typically, the dry cleaner operator has done nothing egregious in operating his business but has simply run the plant with relatively primitive equipment that discharges small amounts of PCE from the dry cleaning machines into sewer drains. Studies conducted by the state of California have revealed that the PCE which is released from dry cleaning units into sewer lines settles to the bottom of the sewer line and seeps through the line into site soil. PCE can leak through joints and cracks in the line. In addition, PCE, being volatile, turns into a gas and penetrates the sewer line wall even where there are no cracks or openings in the joints. Sewer lines are simply not designed to contain gas. The PCE then travels through the vadose zone to the groundwater.

A 1992 study performed by the Central Valley Regional Water Quality Control Board states:

> Where a source investigation has been done in connection with PCE contamination, the evidence has shown that dry cleaners have degraded the groundwater. The data strongly indicate that leakage through the sewer lines is a major avenue through which PCE is introduced to the subsurface.[92]

There are basically five methods by which PCE can penetrate a sewer line:

- through breaks or cracks in the sewer pipes
- through pipe joints and other connections
- by leaching in liquid form directly through sewer lines into the vadose zone

---

92. Izzo, Victor J., "Dry Cleaners—A Major Source of PCE in Groundwater," approved by the California Regional Water Quality Control Board, Central Valley Region, March 27, 1992.

- by saturating the bottom of the sewer pipe with a high concentration of PCE-containing liquid and then PCE volatilizing from the outer edge of the pipe into the soil
- by penetrating the sewer pipe as a gas

In defending against a dry cleaner's CERCLA action, you must pay careful attention to who owns or controls the sewer lateral connections to the sewer main line. You must also pay attention to who owns, operates, or controls the sewer main line. For instance, in the *West Farm* decision rendered by the Fourth Circuit Court of Appeals,[93] West Farm, a property developer who owned land adjacent to a sewer operated by the Washington Suburban Sanitary Commission (WSSC) for Montgomery and Prince George's Counties in Maryland uncovered the presence of PCE in the groundwater beneath the property while performing an environmental audit. Further testing by West Farm's environmental consultants traced the PCE to adjacent landowner, International Fabricare Institute (IFI), who had been conducting laboratory research with PCE to explore the efficacy of various dry cleaning techniques. IFI and its predecessor had been operating a commercial dry-cleaning facility at the adjoining property for approximately twenty years. During that time IFI's research department analyzed hundreds of PCE samples each year and poured the remnants of samples down a sink drain into a connected sewer line. IFI disposed of approximately three gallons of PCE each year into the sewer line from approximately 1974 to 1992. The PCE entered a sewer lateral connecting IFI's building with a main sewer line owned and operated by WSSC.

Remedial investigations performed by West Farm's environmental consultants revealed high concentrations of PCE to the southeast of the sewer lateral, moving with the direction of groundwater flow at the site. To confirm the sources of contamination, West Farm served a subpoena upon WSSC to perform a video camera probe inspection of the sewer lines owned and operated by WSSC. The video probe investigation revealed numerous flaws along the length of the sewer line—including open joints, improper alignment resulting in sags in the line and offset joints, cracks, broken pipes, improperly installed gaskets, and improper manhole construction.

Consequently, West Farm filed a CERCLA action against IFI and WSSC as joint co-defendants. The district court granted West Farm's motion for summary judgment against WSSC and IFI on its CERCLA claims, and the court of appeals upheld the judgment, ruling specifically that a POTW is a "facility" as the term is understood in the CERCLA context;

---

93. *West Farm Associates v. Washington Suburban Sanitary Commission* (4th Cir. 1995) 66 F.3d 669.

that the PCE leaking from WSSC's sewers was released within the meaning of CERCLA; and that WSSC did not meet its burden of producing a genuine dispute of material fact as to non-causation. As such, *West Farm* demonstrates that state, county, or local agencies owning, controlling, or operating sewer systems are viable CERCLA defendants if their activities cause or contribute to a hazardous release.[94]

It should be noted here that often, the various sewer line connections in a shopping center or dry-cleaning facility are owned by the shopping center itself. As such, the shopping center or landlord has a common law duty to maintain the sewer lines and to keep them free of fissures, leaks, and holes. The lease itself, under the repair clause, often contains a covenant to this effect. Therefore, as a part of the site investigation, it may be worthwhile to hire a Roto-Rooter-type plumber to perform a video probe of the dry-cleaning facility sewer line and the shopping center's main line. This is not as expensive as one might expect.

In addition to CERCLA liability, public entities may be liable under such common law theories as negligence and dangerous condition for failing to use reasonable care in the construction, maintenance, and operation of sewers or landfills. The only governmental immunity defense that a public entity has against a claim for negligence or dangerous condition is one of "design immunity" under Govt. Code § 830.6. This defense, however, requires that the governmental entity show a causal relationship between the design and the accident.[95] Where the negligence or dangerous condition has resulted from an independent cause, the design immunity defense will not apply.

Design immunity is limited to a design-caused accident. Put another way, it does not immunize against liability caused by negligence independent of design, even though independent negligence is only a concurring proximate cause of the accident.[96] For instance, where a county has designed a landfill in compliance with state waste discharge requirements, and has also designed percolation retention basins ("catchment basins") to protect against overflows of liquid contaminants from the landfill which may occur as a result of storm water runoff, the county may be liable for the flooding of adjacent property

---

94. *US v. Smuggler-Durant Min. Corp.* (D. Colo. 1993) 823 F.Supp. 873; Cf. *Lincoln Properties, Ltd. v. Higgins* (E.D. Cal. 1992) 823 F.Supp. 1528, 1542-43 (holding county sewer authority entitled to innocent landowner defense where County "took reasonable precautions to prevent releases," and "no evidence [existed] that the county could or should have foreseen the releases.")

95. *Muffett v. Royster* (1983) 147 Cal.App.3d 289, 306; *John Higgins v. State of California* (1997) 54 Cal. App.4th 177.

96. *Mozzetti v. City of Brisbane* (1977) 67 Cal.App.3d 565, 575.

where its failure to properly operate and maintain the catchment basins has reduced their capacity and caused an overflow damaging and contaminating adjacent property.

A dangerous condition claim may be asserted where the condition of public property has caused an injury to adjacent property or to the persons using such adjacent property. Government Code § 830(a) defines "dangerous condition" as "a condition of property that creates a substantial (as distinguished from a minor, trivial, or insignificant) risk of injury when such property or adjacent property is used with due care in a manner in which it is reasonably foreseeable that it will be used." The term "such property or adjacent property" includes the condition of public property that may extend beyond its boundaries and be a hazard to persons or property nearby.[97]

For instance, assume a landfill owned and operated by a county or city has physically changed, or is flawed, damaged, or deteriorated. Assume further that such property has become potentially dangerous to reasonably foreseeable users of adjacent property, even when used with due care, and the county or city entity has had actual notice of the dangerous or defective condition a sufficient time before the injuries occurred and could have taken reasonable measures to protect against such injuries but failed to do so. In this case, the governmental entity may be liable where adjacent property has been flooded by drainage water and contaminated with hazardous waste and hazardous substances because of the creation of such a dangerous or defective condition.

97. See *Milligan v. City of Laguna Beach* (1983) 34 Cal.3d 829 (trees on city property fell on plaintiffs' residence on adjacent property); *Mozzetti v. City of Brisbane*, supra, 67 Cal.App.3d 565 (defective drainage and street improvement project diverted water to adjacent property).

Chapter VI:

The Challenge of Early Mediation

If you are reading this chapter with an especially keen interest and a slightly furrowed brow, it is probably safe to say that the various threshold strategies discussed in the preceding chapters did not allow you to find a quick exit from the threat of pending litigation. Alternatively, you may have been compelled to file a lawsuit because of statute of limitations issues, or because you ran afoul of the difficult hurdle of "claim versus suit" insurance coverage.

Fear not! If you have a ballpark estimate of what the damages are, the best thing you can do is to give serious thought to submitting the case to early mediation. After the lawyer and the litigation consultant have projected the range of damages that are at issue in the case, the lawyer needs to sit down and figure out what the litigation budget projection will be. This is something that will be required by the client and/or the liability insurer paying for the defense, whether mediation is pursued or not.

Once the anticipated daily activity, discovery, law and motion, expert, and trial preparation costs are totaled, it should be assumed that the complete litigation budget projection for the typical environmental case will add up to a substantial six figure sum. When the damages at issue are weighed against the anticipated litigation costs, in most instances you will see the benefit of attempting early mediation.

Are you a wimp if you or your counsel calls up the other side to propose that the case be mediated before the parties incur any further legal fees? No, if you know your case and have completed your early assessment of weighing projected damages[98] against anticipated litigation costs. You will be offering a challenging opportunity from a position of strength, not weakness. If the other parties turn down the invitation, they will be second-guessing you throughout the rest of the case as they try to figure out what it is you know that has eluded them.

Alternative Dispute Resolution (ADR), or mediation, is as old as mankind. There is nothing magical about it, except for the notion that because of the high costs involved in environmental litigation, it is far more preferable to mediate an environmental case than to try it—unless the issue is extremely simple, or the opposing parties are uncompromising to a fault. Even in situations where it would be appropriate to try a case, any environmental lawyer with common sense will worry that the judge or jury will not understand his experts or follow the logical sequence of events which will be critical to understanding the client's case.

A recent study conducted by Cornell University found that of the 88% of the nation's largest corporations that had used mediation within the last three years, 81% considered mediation more satisfactory than litigation, and approximately 90% of the companies found that mediation was less costly than litigation. In that same study, nearly half of the survey respondents also indicated that they lacked confidence in the arbitrators and mediators they hired, and almost 30% of the respondents questioned the qualifications of those who arbitrated or mediated their disputes.[99] In other words, notwithstanding the frequent misgivings they may have had about their individual mediators, these heavy hitters remain overwhelmingly satisfied with mediation as an ADR mechanism.

---

98. Your damage assessment should also establish whether attorneys' fees may be recoverable by virtue of a contested lease or stock transfer provision or an operative state or federal statute. In this regard, as a general principle, it should be noted that attorneys' fees are not recoverable under CERCLA. See *Key Tronic Corp. v. United States* (1994) 511 U.S. 809, 114 S.Ct. 1960. Attorneys' fees, however, are discretionary with the court and may be awarded to the prevailing party in a RCRA action. See *Kasza v. Browner* (D. Nev. 1996) 932 F.Supp. 254. Attorneys' fees may also be recoverable pursuant to certain clauses in any leases that may be at issue or under other state law theories.

99. See "Mediation Madness: Dissatisfied Lawyers Are Rushing into The ADR Business," *California Lawyer* (July 17, 1997).

A. Early Mediation Possibilities

1. Tolling Agreements and Litigation Stays

If the parties are determined to make a good faith effort to resolve the litigation by way of early mediation—but know that they are saddled with a somewhat complex case that will require further evaluation, extensive briefing, and a number of mediation sessions—they may opt to enter into a tolling agreement whereby all parties agree to forebear litigating the matter while they try to resolve it through mediation. As a part of the tolling agreement, without waiving defenses such as statute of limitations, the parties will agree that the period encompassed by the tolling agreement will not count. The termination of the tolling agreement should be triggered by any party's unilateral decision to rescind it.

If you're the plaintiff, because of the various statutory requirements for bringing cases to trial within a limited time frame, you may also need to dismiss the pending action without prejudice. The tolling agreement will allow you to refile the suit without compromising any aspect of the claims stated as of the date of the initial filing. Normally, the tolling agreement will provide that the action can be recommenced within a certain number of days after any party receives notice of withdrawal from the agreement from any other party, but that the tolling agreement itself will not be null and void until a certain period of time has passed after any party has withdrawn.

A less complicated and more straightforward approach may be to simply enter a stipulation between all counsel to stay the case while the parties try to resolve it through early mediation. The stipulation will be meaningless if not accompanied by a court order wherein the judge endorses the concept and agrees to put the case on hold for the amount of time requested or for either a shorter or longer period depending on the court's opinion of what is needed. Sometimes, either the tolling agreement or litigation stay fails because one or more parties in a multi-party case refuse to agree to the stay or tolling.

2. Further Remedial Investigation

If the parties concur that additional PRPs may exist, with or without a tolling agreement, they can form their own mini-PRP group to perform an additional site investigation. The work-product privilege of their consultants will, of course, be waived for this limited purpose, but the benefits are twofold. First, remedial investigation expenses are minimized because the parties share in the expense (usually on an equal-shares basis). Second, if the parties' joint hunch is borne out, new guests will be invited to the settlement table to fund the cleanup. If both sides of the dispute cannot agree upon the need for further investigation, often the defendants will form a group themselves to perform a further site investigation.

Ideally, the tolling and further investigation approaches will precede the early mediation. Otherwise, the early mediation will probably never happen or will serve as nothing more than an exercise in futility if allowed to proceed.

B. The Importance of Using an Environmental Mediator

Ideally, the mediator should possess the legal knowledge of the relevant area of law. They should also be a legal practitioner or a retired judge. Environmental cases have their own special nuances, terms of art, laws, statutes, and regulations. Even the simplest environmental cases are, at heart, complex to the uninitiated. It is an absolute waste of time to use a mediator who has no knowledge of environmental litigation. Such a mediator will know nothing about the law and will have no understanding of the technical aspects of the case.

Whether the mediator is a lawyer or judge, however, the parties should be careful to inquire about exactly what the "environmental" label means, and to review the mediator's biographical profile. Often, the would-be mediator has been involved only in environmental insurance coverage cases. Although the same issues can sometimes arise in both liability and coverage cases, environmental coverage cases are normally far less technical than liability cases and do not usually interpret the same laws. Therefore, although environmental insurance coverage experience in a mediator is helpful, the mediator must be knowledgeable in both liability and coverage to be potentially effective. This way, they will understand the issues in the liability case. They will also be able to communicate with both the carrier representatives who insure the parties and the insurance coverage counsel (mostly for the carriers, but sometimes for the insured) who will often be participants in the mediation process.

C. Mediation Techniques

The good thing about mediation is that it is basically voluntary and non-binding. In some instances, a trial judge may order the parties to mediate their dispute; but beyond some initial prodding, it is up to the parties themselves to reach an agreement. Unlike an arbitrator, whose task is to render a judgment, the mediator's function is to help the parties reach agreement on their dispute and to assist the parties in coming up with creative solutions to resolve their problems. To be effective, the mediator must do more than handholding. They must be tough at times. The effective mediator usually combines two contrasting techniques in dealing with the parties: the evaluative approach and the facilitative approach.

The evaluative approach is logical and objective. With this method, the mediator evaluates and critiques the strengths and weaknesses of each party's position. Retired judges tend to feel most comfortable with this somewhat autocratic method. The facilitative approach is non-judgmental. The mediator who uses this approach in its undiluted form merely assists each party in telling its version of the story.

Using either approach in isolation can be the death knell of what could otherwise be a fruitful mediation. For instance, if the mediator, in a roundtable discussion with all parties, focuses entirely on a legal analysis of why a particular statute of limitations defense or mitigation of damages argument advanced by one of the defendants is flawed and without merit, the plaintiff will be completely uncompromising in its position, whether the mediator is right or wrong.

If, however, the mediator expresses his informed opinion concerning the strengths and weaknesses of each party's position—in confidential, closed-door sessions with each individual party and that party's counsel—they may enable the parties to more accurately assess their positions and pave the way towards compromise. In other words, the parties usually agree that they would like to settle their dispute and avoid needless litigation costs; but in a visceral sense, they do not always accept the idea that they must compromise unless a mediator can intercede with an evaluative approach that serves as a wake-up call. This is an objective, quasi-judicial function which foreshadows what the result will be with a judge or jury if the case does not settle.

The mediator will convey most of the evaluative information from the standpoint of the opposing party, serving as the messenger. Then, if necessary, he will let the parties know in confidence if he agrees with their individual positions. The seasoned mediator will go one step further as a facilitator to suggest new approaches or creative solutions that the parties may not have previously considered.

Chapter VII:

The Law Game: The Development of an Initial Legal Strategy

A. Statute of Limitations

As should be evident by the discussion which follows, for the most part, the statutes of limitations are so expansive and flexible for CERCLA and RCRA claims that the defense does not usually have much value under these two federal acts. The statute of limitations defense is, however, alive and well for California state law claims.

1. CERCLA Claims

Pursuant to CERCLA § 113(g)(2), 42 U.S.C. § 9613(g)(2), claims to recover costs for a "removal action," as the term is defined by 42 U.S.C. § 9601(23), must be brought within three years after completion of the cleanup or removal of hazardous substances.

Suits seeking recovery of costs for a "remedial action," pursuant to CERCLA § 113(g)(2), 42 U.S.C. § 9613(g)(2), must be brought within six years after initiation of physical onsite construction of the remedial action. The exception is if the remedial action is initiated within three years after completion of the removal action, then costs incurred in the removal action may be recovered in the cost recovery action brought for reimbursement of "remedial" costs, as such costs are defined by 42 U.S.C. § 9601(24).

Finally, an action for contribution brought pursuant to CERCLA § 113(f), 42 U.S.C. § 9613(f), must be brought no more than three years after entry of judgment, entry of the judicially approved settlement or issuance of an administrative order or de minimis settlement, pursuant to 42 U.S.C. § 9613(g)(3). Subrogation actions arising by virtue of CERCLA claim payments must also be commenced within three years after payment of those claims pursuant to 42 U.S.C. § 9613(g)(4).

A 1997 decision from the Third Circuit Court of Appeals, *New Castle County v. Halliburton NUS Corp.* (3d Cir. 1997) 111 F.3d 1116 demonstrates that the statute of limitations defense on contribution actions is alive and well. The case arose from efforts to clean up the Tybouts Corner Landfill, a hazardous substance site located in Delaware. In 1980, the United States had filed suit against New Castle County, the owner and operator of the landfill. On April 19, 1989, the EPA entered into a series of consent decrees with New Castle County and other PRPs, requiring them to finance and implement remedial action at the landfill. Prior to entry of the consent decrees, the EPA contracted with Halliburton NUS Corp. (NUS) to perform a remedial investigation / feasibility study to determine appropriate response actions. NUS installed several monitoring wells in areas where refuse had been placed during the landfill's operation. One of the wells was installed to assess a clay strata separating a shallow formation containing groundwater impacted by landfill material, and a deeper formation containing groundwater used as drinking water by New Castle County. NUS reported that the clay formation was missing in the vicinity of the monitoring well.

According to the county, NUS improperly constructed the well in question and opened a "window" between the two groundwater formations. The county learned of NUS's alleged mistakes in a report dated October 28, 1991. However, the county did not file its contribution action against NUS until October 26, 1993—nearly three and a half years after New Castle entered into the consent decrees with the EPA. NUS moved for summary judgment on the County's CERCLA claims on two grounds: (1) that the county, as a potentially responsible party under CERCLA § 107(a), was not entitled to bring a CERCLA § 107 action against another potentially responsible party; and (2) that the county was limited to a CERCLA § 113(f)(1) contribution action, which was barred by that section's three-year statute of limitations.

As noted above, cost recovery suits for reimbursement of the costs of remedial actions are typically governed by a six-year statute of limitations. Contribution actions under

CERCLA § 113, on the other hand, are governed by a three-year statute of limitations. Thus, NUS's motion for summary judgment turned on the court agreeing with both prongs of its argument. After first holding that New Castle was limited to a contribution claim under CERCLA § 113, the district court also determined that New Castle's contribution cause of action accrued on the date of the consent decrees and was therefore barred by the three-year statute of limitations.

Appealing to the Third Circuit, the county argued two points. First, that pursuant to the discovery rule, its contribution claim did not accrue until October 28, 1991, when it discovered NUS's alleged negligence while reviewing the report NUS had submitted to EPA. Second, that the statute of limitations was equitably tolled.

The Third Circuit Court of Appeals rejected both of New Castle's arguments. First, as to the discovery rule, the Court of Appeals held that "the discovery rule does not delay the running of the statute of limitations until a plaintiff is aware of all of the facts necessary to bring its cause of action. Under the discovery rule, a claim accrues upon awareness of actual injury, not upon awareness that the injury constitutes a legal wrong."[100] The Third Circuit further held that the discovery rule does not delay the accrual of a cause of action until a plaintiff has identified every party who may be liable on its claim.[101] For the Third Circuit, it was "sufficient that New Castle was aware that its injury was caused in part by another person's conduct." At the time of the consent decree, New Castle County was aware that "other persons were partially responsible for the landfill's condition." Prior to 1989, the county had brought several contribution actions against other PRPs and was also aware that NUS's activity and report played a significant role in the determination of New Castle's potential liability at the site. As such, on April 19, 1989, the date of the consent decrees, the Court of Appeals held that the county was aware of both its injury and the immediate cause of that injury. Consequently, the Court of Appeals agreed with the district court that the discovery rule did not render New Castle's § 113 claim timely.

Concerning equitable tolling, the Third Circuit Court of Appeals explained that the doctrine may apply in the following circumstances: (1) where the defendant has actively misled the plaintiff respecting the plaintiff 's cause of action; (2) where the plaintiff in some extraordinary way has been prevented from asserting his or her rights; or (3) where the plaintiff has asserted his or her rights in a timely manner, but in the wrong forum.[102]

---

100. *New Castle County*, supra, 111 F.3d at 1125.

101. Ibid.

102. Ibid.; *Oshiver v. Levin, Fishbein, Sedran & Berman* (3d Cir. 1994) 38 F.3d 1380, 1387.

The county relied on the second option under the doctrine of equitable tolling, contending that the difficult implementation of the remedial action at the landfill constituted an extraordinary circumstance preventing it from asserting its rights in a timely fashion. The Third Circuit Court of Appeals did not agree, characterizing the county's delay as "excusable neglect," at best. Because excusable neglect is insufficient to invoke equitable tolling, the Third Circuit concluded that no extraordinary circumstance had prevented New Castle County from filing its lawsuit, and held that its contribution claim was barred by the three-year statute of limitations.

2. RCRA Claims

No specific statute of limitations exists for claims brought under RCRA, although it has been argued that the federal tort claims statute of limitations may apply. See 28 U.S.C. § 2415(a), (b). The most critical and obvious statute of limitations that now applies to all private party suits under RCRA, pursuant to the US Supreme Court's decision in *Mehrig v. KFC Western, Inc.* (1996) 516 U.S. 479, is that an action may be commenced under RCRA only while the threat of "imminent" harm exists from the contamination problem. If the cleanup has already been completed, the private party plaintiff will not be able to obtain a mandatory or prohibitory injunction covering any past cleanup efforts, because the Supreme Court has held that RCRA does not afford restitutionary relief but only injunctive relief. In other words, the court action must be filed and a mandatory injunction requiring cleanup must be sought before undertaking any cleanup of the contaminated site.

3. State Law Claims

The defendant may also have statute of limitations defenses to state law claims for breach of contract, permanent or continuing nuisance, trespass, or fraud.

a. Contract Claims

In California, the statute of limitations for breach of a written contract is four years.[103]

103. Cal. Code Civ. Proc. § 337.1.

Generally, contract causes of action accrue at the date of injury.[104] Where, however, the breach is committed in secret, and the harm extending from the breach will not be reasonably discoverable by the plaintiff until a future time, the "discovery rule" will apply.[105] Under the discovery rule, a cause of action will be deemed to accrue when the plaintiff "discovers or should have discovered all facts essential to his cause of action."[106] To invoke the discovery rule, a plaintiff must plead facts sufficient to convince the trial judge that delayed discovery was justified.[107] Such facts include the plaintiff 's lack of knowledge and lack of means of obtaining knowledge, and how and when the plaintiff actually discovered the facts.[108] If the plaintiff did discover or could have discovered the contamination at issue more than four years before bringing the claim for breach of contract, the defendant may have grounds to plead the statute of limitations.

b. Permanent Nuisance and Permanent Trespass

Pursuant to California Code of Civil Procedure § 338(b), there is a three-year statute of limitations period for property damage claims. As with breach of contract, California courts apply a "discovery" rule to determine when the limitations period starts to run. As summarized by the Court of Appeal:

> The statute of limitations begins to run when the plaintiff suspects or should suspect that his or her injury was caused by wrongdoing when the plaintiff has notice of information or circumstances that would put a reasonable person on inquiry. The plaintiff need not be aware of the specific facts necessary to establish the claim. These facts can be determined during

104. *April Enterprises, Inc. v. KTTV* (1983) 147 Cal.App.3d 805, 832.

105. Id. at 832.

106. Id. at 826.

107. Id. at 832.

108. *Lee v. Escrow Consultants, Inc.* (1989) 210 Cal.App.3d 915, 920.

> pretrial discovery. Once the plaintiff suspects wrongdoing and therefore has an incentive to sue, he or she must decide whether to file suit or sit on his or her rights. When a suspicion exists, the plaintiff must go find the facts; he or she cannot wait for the facts to find him or her.[109]

In other words, under the discovery rule, the limitations period begins when:

> a person becomes aware of facts which would make a reasonably prudent person suspicious, [at which time] he or she has a duty to investigate further and is charged with knowledge of matters which would have been revealed by such an investigation.[110]

In *Mangini I*, the Court of Appeal addressed the application of the "discovery rule" exception to the statute of limitations and stated:

> Thus, in 1984, more than three years before filing the complaint, plaintiffs knew the following facts: (1) the recorded lease gave notice that defendant had engaged in activities of a potentially hazardous nature on their land [citations]; (2) the Department of Justice investigated defendant's practices regarding disposal of hazardous waste in the area; and (3) defendant asked plaintiffs for permission to inspect their property.
>
> Whether any of these three facts in isolation would be sufficient to impart notice is open to dispute. However, the *combination of these facts together establish as a matter of law* that, when defendant contacted plaintiffs in 1984, plaintiffs had sufficient information to put them on notice of the possibility

---

109. *San Francisco Unified School District v. W.R.Grace & Co.* (1995) 37 Cal.App.4th 1318, 1326-1327, citing *Jolly v. Eli Lilly & Co.* (1988) 44 Cal.3d 1103, 1110-1111, 1114.

110. *Mangini v. Aerojet-General Corp.* (1991) 230 Cal.App.3d 1125, 1150 (*Mangini I*).

> that defendant had dumped hazardous waste on their land.[111]

Neither actual discovery nor "subjective suspicion" is required.[112] The limitations period simply "begins once the plaintiff has notice or information of circumstances to put a reasonable person on inquiry."[113] For example, in *Mortkowitz v. Texaco, Inc.* (N.D. Cal. 1994) 842 F.Supp. 1232, the plaintiff site owners did not become aware that a pipe union (i.e., a pipe coupling) in an underground storage system was leaking until nearly six years after the plaintiffs had purchased the underground storage tank system from a prior lessee. Nonetheless, applying California law, the District Court held that the statute of limitations had run because the knowledge that the property had been utilized as a gasoline station for a number of years "should have put Plaintiffs on inquiry about possible soil contamination notwithstanding the duty of inquiry imposed upon them by law."[114] Specifically citing *Mangini I*, the District Court held:

> The *combination* of Plaintiffs' *knowledge of the age of the underground tank system* along with the *statutory duty of inquiry* imposed upon all owners and operators of underground tanks *establishes as a matter of law* that Plaintiffs should have been on notice of the possibility that their property may have been contaminated and that Texaco may have caused some or all of the contamination. See, e.g. [*Mangini I*], supra. Therefore, the statute of limitations on Plaintiffs' claims for negligence, permanent nuisance, permanent trespass, and strict liability began to run no later than July, 1985, and expired in July 1988, nearly two years before Plaintiffs filed suit in April 1990.[115]

---

111. Id. at 1152-1153, emphasis added.

112. Id. at 1150.

113. Id.; *California Sansome Co. v. U.S. Gypsum Co.* (N.D. Cal. 1993) 819 F.Supp. 878, 881 [opining California Supreme Court would decide under "discovery rule" that "[t]he limitations period began to run on plaintiffs at the point of 'suspicion,' when plaintiffs were first put 'on inquiry,' despite the fact that additional time may reasonably have been necessary to actually conduct the inquiry and confirm the suspicions."]

114. *Mortkowitz v. Texaco, Inc.* (N.D. Cal. 1994) 842 F.Supp. 1232, 1240.

115, Id. at 1240-1241, emphasis added.

In *Wilshire Westwood v. Atlantic Richfield* (1993) 20 Cal.App.4th, 732, 740, a consultant knew but failed to advise that gasoline odors were present on property, and the Court of Appeal affirmed summary judgment of negligence and strict liability on the statute of limitations, because the plaintiff had "'presumptive knowledge' so as to commence the running of the statute . . . [where plaintiff] has the opportunity to obtain knowledge from sources open to his investigation."

Inasmuch as the "discovery rule" is meant to ameliorate the harshness of applying the statute of limitations to the blamelessly ignorant plaintiff, the rule allows the plaintiff to plead facts which show the time and manner of discovery and the inability to have made earlier discovery despite reasonable diligence. Both the *Mangini I* and *Mortkowitz* courts, however, have made it clear that where there is a combination of facts that should have put the plaintiff on notice of their injury, the statute of limitations begins to run as a matter of law.

Therefore, where facts like those discussed in the preceding California authorities exist, the defendant may have grounds to file a demurrer or motion to dismiss on the grounds that the negligence, permanent nuisance, or permanent trespass claims are time barred by the three-year statute of limitations set forth in Code of Civil Procedure § 338(b).

One unusual situation to keep in mind is where the "construction defect statute," California Code of Civil Procedure § 337.15, is applied to state law claims involving federally regulated hazardous substances. California Code of Civil Procedure § 337.15 provides that where a plaintiff seeks to recover for damage to real property caused by a latent defect in the construction of an improvement to the property, "no action may be brought . . . more than ten years after the substantial completion of the . . . improvement." On its face, it appears that Code of Civil Procedure § 337.15 imposes an absolute ten-year bar on latent defect claims based on the date of "substantial completion," regardless of when the claim is discovered. However, where the claim concerns damage caused by hazardous substances regulated under CERCLA, that law provides, in pertinent part:

> In the case of any action brought under state law for personal injury, or property damages, which are caused or contributed to by exposure to any hazardous substance, or pollutant or contaminant, released into the environment from a facility, if the applicable limitations period for such action (as specified in the State statute of limitations or under common law) provides a commencement date which is earlier than the federally-

> required commencement date, *such period shall commence at the federally-required commencement date in lieu of the date specified in such State statute.*[116]

CERCLA defines "federally required commencement date" as the "date the plaintiff knew (or reasonably should have known) that the personal injury or property damages were caused or contributed to by the hazardous substance or pollutant or contaminant concerned."[117] Consequently, California Code of Civil Procedure § 337.15 is trumped by the federal discovery rule and will not apply where the contamination claim pertaining to CERCLA-regulated hazardous substances is discovered (within the meaning of the discovery rule) more than ten years after substantial completion of the improvement. The improvement, of course, can be a manufacturing plant, a tank farm or underground storage tank facility, a piping system related to an underground storage tank facility, or other such facilities constructed for the purpose of storing or using CERCLA-regulated hazardous substances.[118] Whatever the improvement may be, the federal discovery rule will preemptively control if the CERCLA contamination claim would otherwise be barred by Code of Civil Procedure § 337.15.

c. Fraud or Negligent Misrepresentation Claims

Code of Civil Procedure § 338(d) establishes a three-year statute of limitations for "an action for relief on the ground of fraud or mistake." The cause of action accrues upon "discovery by the aggrieved party of the facts constituting the fraud or mistake."[119]

"Failure to discover all the details of a fraud does not prevent the statute from running."[120] The statute of limitations period under Code of Civil Procedure § 338(d)

---

116. CERCLA § 309, 42 U.S.C. § 9658(a)(1), emphasis added.

117. 42 U.S.C. § 9658(b)(4)(A).

118. See *Angeles Chemical Co. v. Spencer & Jones* (1996) 44 Cal.App.4th 112.

119. Code Civ. Proc. § 338(d).

120. *Turner v. Lunquist* (9th Cir. 1967) 377 F.2d 44, 48 (following California law in interpreting prior Code

"commences when the plaintiff discovered or could have discovered the fraud with the exercise of reasonable diligence."[121] Therefore, if the plaintiff has discovered the contamination present at the site more than three years prior to the filing of the claim for fraud, intentional misrepresentation, or negligent misrepresentation, or if the complaint on its face shows that the plaintiff had the alleged facts constituting the fraud in his or her possession more than three years before the filing of the action, the defendant may assert that the claims for fraud, intentional misrepresentation or negligent misrepresentation are time barred pursuant to California Code of Civil Procedure § 338(d).

d. Continuing Nuisance or Continuing Trespass Claims

It may be difficult, if not impossible, to obtain an adjudication that a continuing nuisance or continuing trespass claim is barred by the statute of limitations based on the face of the pleading alone. However, if numerous studies have already been performed on the site that will allow for a quick technical assessment of the contamination at issue, it may be possible to file an early motion for summary judgment or summary adjudication after answering the complaint. For this reason, although motions for summary judgment normally come further down the line, here we include an analysis of how a determination on continuing nuisance or trespass may be made as a matter of law. Where the nature of the contamination is static and not continuing, and the contamination does not appear to have the potential to migrate, a strong argument may be made that the alleged nuisance or trespass should be characterized as permanent, causing the statute of limitations to begin operating. Thus, the defendant must first obtain a ruling that the nuisance should be characterized as permanent rather than continuing; then, the defendant must also show that the statute of limitations applicable to permanent tort-based claims, Code of Civil Procedure § 338(b), would bar any claims of permanent nuisance or permanent trespass.

The salient feature of a continuing nuisance or continuing trespass is that its impact "may vary over time, that is, an impact that will repeatedly disturb the property or which

---

of Civil Procedure § 338(4)).

121. *Admiralty Fund v. Hugh Johnson & Co.* (9th Cir. 1982) 677 F.2d 1301, 1309; see also *Parsons v. Tickner* (1995) 31 Cal.App.4th 1513, 1525.

may gradually increase over time."[122] Contamination "may be shown to be a continuing nuisance by evidence that the contaminants continue to migrate through land and groundwater causing new and additional damage on a continuous basis."[123]

The basic test for determining whether a nuisance is permanent or continuing is the "abatability test" recently adopted by the California Supreme Court in *Mangini v. Aerojet-General Corp.* (1996) 12 Cal.4th 1087 (*Mangini II*) wherein the court held "abatable" to mean that "the nuisance can be remedied at reasonable cost by a reasonable means."[124] It is the plaintiff's burden to present "evidence that the injury is capable of being abated and that the cost of abatement is 'reasonable.'"[125] Even where the contamination is alleged to be unlawful or exceeding government standards, this does not automatically establish the nuisance to be continuing rather than permanent, especially where a plaintiff does not seek abatement but only monetary damages.[126]

Therefore, because the defendant must assume the burden of proof on the motion for summary adjudication, the defendant must present convincing extrinsic evidence and expert declarations to illustrate (1) that the nature of the contamination is static and unvarying, not continuing; (2) that the plaintiff failed to abate the nuisance at a reasonable cost; and (3) that the means employed by the plaintiff to remediate the nuisance were unreasonable. Where the cost of remediation far exceeds the actual detriment that the plaintiff would have suffered if the property had not been remediated, the defendant may be able to make a prima facie showing that the costs incurred were unreasonable. In addition, where the plaintiff has not followed appropriate steps in performing site remediation activities, this failure may enable the defendant to show that the means used to abate the contamination were per se unreasonable.

---

122. *Beck Development Co., Inc. v. Southern Pacific Transportation Co.* (1996) 44 Cal.App.4th 1160.

123. Id. at 557.

124. *Mangini v. Aerojet-General Corp.* (1996) 12 Cal.4th 1087, 1103.

125. Id. at 1104.

126. Id. at 1102-1103.

B. Other CERCLA Defenses to Liability

1. Contribution

CERCLA § 107(a) provides that an owner or operator of a facility or a generator or transporter of hazardous substances shall be liable for costs of removal or remediation incurred by the United States, a state, or an Indian tribe, and for any other necessary response costs incurred by any other person consistent with the National Contingency Plan. While § 107(a) does not expressly provide for joint and several liability, § 107(a) has been interpreted to hold PRPs strictly liable, as well as jointly and severally liable, to the government or to innocent persons if there was a release or threat of a release of a hazardous substance at a facility and the government or innocent person incurred necessary response costs consistent with the National Contingency Plan.[127]

Liability under CERCLA § 113(f), however, has been held to be several only. Under § 113(f) "any person may seek contribution from any other person who is liable or potentially liable under section 9607(a)," which "shall be governed by Federal law." Under CERCLA § 113 (f), the federal district judge "may allocate response costs among liable parties using such equitable factors as the court determines are appropriate."[128] As such, the Court has wide discretion to do whatever it thinks is necessary to achieve justice between the parties so that no party will end up paying more than its equitable share.

While not a knockout punch or complete defense, bringing a contribution action under CERCLA is often the best defense that a liable party has, especially if the liable party has been sued for cost recovery under CERCLA. There are two questions. First, can a PRP who voluntarily incurs response costs, who has not been sued under CERCLA, and who has not entered into an administrative settlement seek contribution under CERCLA § 113? Strangely, the answer was no, at least initially, according to the US Supreme Court.[129] But fear not: just 3 years later, in *US v. Atlantic Research Corp.* (2007) 551 U.S. 128, the Supremes unanimously ruled that individual and corporate parties who voluntarily perform

---

127. 42 U.S.C. § 9607(a).

128. 42 U.S.C. § 9613 (f).

129. See *Cooper Industries, Inc. v. Aviall Services, Inc.* (2004) 543 U.S. 157.

hazardous waste cleanups have the right to recover their costs from other responsible parties. But it's complicated. A liable party can pursue a contribution claim under Section 113 and a Section 107 claim if that party has actually incurred response costs. However, if the party did not incur response costs, the party is limited to a contribution claim.

2. Innocent Landowner Defense

CERCLA § 9607(b)(3) provides a complete "third-party defense" to CERCLA liability where the defendant can show, by a preponderance of the evidence, that the release of hazardous substances was caused solely by "an action or omission of a third party other than an employee or agent of the defendant, or than [sic] one whose act or omission occurs in connection with a contractual relationship . . . with the defendant . . ."[130] Section 9601(35)(A) states that "the term 'contractual relationship,' for the purposes of section 9607(b)(3) of this title includes . . . land contracts, deeds, or other instruments transferring title or possession," unless the purchaser of the property can establish what is commonly called the "innocent landowner defense."[131] The innocent landowner defense requires the purchaser to establish, by a preponderance of evidence, that at the time it acquired the facility it "did not know and had no reason to know that any hazardous substance which is the subject of the release . . . was disposed of on, in, or at the facility."[132]

To establish that it "did not know and had no reason to know that any hazardous substance . . . was disposed of . . . at the facility," a purchaser of contaminated property must show that, at the time of acquisition, it undertook "all appropriate inquiry into the previous ownership and uses of the property consistent with good commercial or customary practices in an effort to minimize liability."[133] In evaluating the "all appropriate inquiry" element, the court must take into account the purchaser's state of knowledge at the time of acquisition and weigh various factors, including: (1) the specialized knowledge or experience of the buyer; (2) the relationship of the purchase price to the value of the property

---

130. 42 U.S.C. § 9607(b)(3).

131. 42 U.S.C. § 9601(35)(A)(i).

132. Ibid.

133. 42 U.S.C. § 9601(35)(B).

if uncontaminated; (3) commonly known or reasonably ascertainable information about the property; (4) the obviousness of the presence or likely presence of contamination at the property; and (5) the ability to detect such contamination by appropriate inspection.[134]

Thus, to successfully assert the "innocent landowner" defense, the defendant must establish several things:

- The contaminated property was acquired by defendant after the release or disposal of hazardous substances occurred.
- The defendant neither knew nor should have known the property was contaminated with hazardous substances at the time defendant acquired the property.
- The defendant failed to discover the contamination present at the property despite having conducted all appropriate "due diligence" into previous ownership and uses of the property at the time of acquisition.

According to the Act's legislative history, the innocent landowner defense "is intended to clarify and confirm that under limited circumstances, landowners who acquire property without knowing of any contamination at the site and without reason to know of any contamination . . . may have a defense to liability under section 107. . . *if such persons satisfy the remaining requirements of CERCLA § 107(b)(3)*. A person who acquires property through a land contract . . . may assert that an act or omission of a third party should not be considered to have occurred in connection with a contractual relationship as identified in section 107(b) and therefore is not a bar to the defense."[135]

If you have substantial evidence that you or your client made all appropriate inquiries when purchasing the property, and that the client did not know or have reason to know that any hazardous substances were disposed of there, you may be able to prevail with the "innocent landowner" defense in an early motion for summary judgment. For example, if the client purchased the property at full market value, physically inspected the property before making the purchase, and no one touring the property could have known that hazardous releases had occurred there, the defense may be viable.

Up until 2002, however, when the landowner commissioned an environmental study

---

134. Ibid.

135. Conference Report on Superfund Amendments and Reauthorization Act of 1986, H.R. Rep. No. 99-962 (1986) (Conf. Rep.), emphasis added.

which indicated the presence of hazardous substances on the property, the landowner was no longer innocent.[136]

3. Bona Fide Prospective Purchaser Defense

Not to worry—the times they are a changin'. (Or, to quote another Bob Dylan song, we're "Knockin' on Heaven's Door.") The door is no longer closed on property owners who knowingly purchase contaminated property. Although the draconian scope of Section 107(a) (1) of CERCLA, 42 U.S.C. §9607(a), imposes liability upon the current "owner or operator of a . . . facility," in 2002, Congress enacted the Brownfields Amendments to CERCLA which, among other things, provide CERCLA liability protection to "bona fide purchaser" landowners who would otherwise be liable under §107(a)(1) (the "BFPP Defense"). Congress added CERCLA § 107(r), 42 U.S.C. §9607(r), which provides that a "bona fide purchaser" is not liable as an owner or operator under §107(a)(1). It defined a "bona fide purchaser" as a party that "made all appropriate inquiries into the previous ownership and uses of the facility in accordance with generally accepted good commercial and customary standards and practices."[137]

Section 101(35) (B) (iv) (II) of CERCLA, 42 U.S.C. §9601(35) (B) (iv) (II), defines "all appropriate inquiry" as performing a Phase I environmental report consistent with standards adopted by the American Society of Testing and Materials ("ASTM").

Elements of BFPP Defense

A Bona Fide Prospective Purchaser is a person who

1. acquires ownership of the facility after January 11, 2002;
2. establishes by a preponderance of the evidence that all disposal of hazardous substances at the facility occurred before the person acquired the facility;
3. makes all appropriate inquiries into the previous ownership and

136. See *US v. Shell Oil Co.* (C.D. Cal. 1993) 841 F.Supp. 962, 973-974 [Defense rejected where the Court found "overwhelming evidence that not only did [the defendant] have ample reason to know of the presence of hazardous wastes at the country club, it had actual knowledge of that fact prior to its purchase of the Club . . ."].

137. CERCLA § 101(40), 42 U.S.C. §9601(40).

uses of the facility in accordance with generally accepted good commercial and customary standards and practices [section 101(35) (B) (iv) (II) of CERCLA, 42 U.S.C. §9601(35) (B) (iv) (II), defines "all appropriate inquiry" as performing a Phase I environmental report consistent with standards adopted by the American Society of Testing and Materials ("ASTM")];

4. provides all legally required notices with respect to the discovery or release of any hazardous substances at the facility;
5. exercises appropriate care with respect to hazardous substances found at the facility by taking reasonable steps to—
   (I) stop any continuing release;
   (II) prevent any threatened future release; and
   (III) prevent or limit human, environmental, or natural resource exposure to any previously released hazardous substance.
6. provides full cooperation, assistance, and access to persons that are authorized to conduct response actions or natural resource restoration at the facility (including the cooperation and access necessary for the installation, integrity, operation, and maintenance of any complete or partial response actions or natural resource restoration at the facility).
7. complies with any land use restrictions established or relied on in connection with the response action at the facility; and does not impede the effectiveness or integrity of any institutional control employed at the vessel or facility in connection with a response action;
8. complies with any request for information or administrative subpoena issued by regulators; and
9. is not potentially liable, or affiliated with any other person that is potentially liable, for response costs at the facility through— any direct or indirect familial relationship; or any contractual, corporate, or financial relationship (other than a contractual, corporate, or financial relationship that is created by the instruments by which title to the facility is conveyed or financed, by a tenancy, by the instruments by which a leasehold interest in the facility is created, or by a contract for the sale of goods or services); or the result of a reorganization of a business entity that was potentially liable.

4. If There Has Been No Release of Any Hazardous Substance from the Facility into the Environment, It May Be Argued That Liability Has Not Been Triggered under CERCLA

The definition of "covered person" under 42 U.S.C. § 9607(a)(3) encompasses the owner or operator of a "facility," or any person who "arranged with a transporter for transport for disposal" of hazardous substances at a "facility." CERCLA defines "facility" as a "landfill," or "any site or area where a hazardous substance has been deposited, stored, disposed of, or placed, or otherwise come to be located."[138] Liability attaches only to facilities "from which there is a release, or threatened release."[139]

With respect to the language of 42 U.S.C. § 9607(a)(4), it should be noted that, "as courts have observed, Congress intended that [this] language relate not only to § 9607(a)(4), but also to § 9607(a)(1) - (3), but apparently misdrafted the language. See, e.g., *Dedham Water Co. v. Cumberland Farms Dairy, Inc.*, 889 F.2d 1146, 1151 n.4 (1st Cir. 1989); *New York v. Shore Realty Corp.*, 759 F.2d 1032, 1043 n.16 (2nd. Cir. 1985)."[140]

The definition of "release" as set forth at 42 U.S.C. § 9601(22) is as follows: "any spilling, leaking, pumping, pouring, admitting, emptying, discharging, injecting, escaping, leaching, dumping, or disposing into the environment." "Environment" is defined as "navigable waters . . . any other surface water, groundwater, drinking water supply, land surface or subsurface strata or ambient air . . ."[141] For the term "environment" to be something more than mere surplusage, it must have a different meaning from "facility."[142] The CERCLA definition of disposal reflects the intended difference in the terms. Pursuant to 42 U.S.C. § 9601(29), the definition of "disposal" incorporates the meaning of the term

138. 42 U.S.C. § 9601(9).

139. 42 U.S.C. § 9607(a)(4).

140. *US v. Alcan Corp.* (3d Cir 1992) 964 F.2d 252, 257 fn. 4; *Ascon Properties v. Mobil Oil Co.* (9th Cir. 1989) 866 F.2d 1149, 1152.

141. 42 U.S.C. § 9601(8).

142. See *Wilshire Westwood Assoc. v. Atlantic Richfield Co.* (9th Cir. 1989) 881 F.2d 801, 804 [Interpreting CERCLA: "This court must look beyond the express language of a statute where a literal interpretation 'would thwart the purpose of the overall statutory scheme or lead to an absurd result . . . statutes should not be construed to make surplusage of any provision.'"]

provided in section 1004 of the Solid Waste Disposal Act,[143] which defines disposal as:

> The discharge, deposit, injection, dumping, spilling, leaking, or placing of any solid waste or hazardous waste into or on any land or water so that such solid waste or hazardous waste or any constituent thereof may enter the environment or be admitted into the air or discharged into any waters, including groundwaters.[144]

It should also be noted that the definition of "release" excludes any release that results in exposure to persons solely within a workplace.[145] Consistent with this exclusion, the CERCLA definition of environment defines the air as the "ambient air," meaning that it is only a release or threatened release into the atmosphere beyond the site which constitutes a release into the environment.

In similar fashion, for the statute to be reasonable and sensible, it is arguable that the term "land surface" within the definition of environment is intended to mean a "land surface" beyond the site itself, which would mean contamination with a migratory potential evidencing a capability to move into the subsurface strata, groundwater, or ambient air beyond the facility's boundaries.

Consistent with this reasoning, a relatively recent DC Circuit Court of Appeals decision addressed the facility/environment distinction in considering a rule promulgated by the EPA to regulate the reporting requirements for the release of radionuclides (radioactive elements). This decision employed an interpretation of the CERCLA term "release" that the court held "contrary to the express language of CERCLA."[146] The DC Circuit Court held that CERCLA defines a "release" as "the movement of a substance from a facility into

---

143. 42 U.S.C. § 6903(3).

144. The Ninth Circuit Court of Appeals has held that the plain meaning of the term "disposal" dictates that the passive migration of contaminants through the soil or groundwater does not give rise to CERCLA liability where: (1) the contaminants were not disposed of on the property during the owner's period of ownership; and (2) the owner seeking to be relieved of liability has done nothing to exacerbate the contamination. (See *Carson Harbor Village Ltd v. Unocal Corp.* (9th Cir. 2001) 270 F.3d 863.)

145. CERCLA § 101(22), 42 U.S.C. § 9601(22).

146. *Fertilizer Institute v. US EPA* (D.C. Cir. 1991) 935 F.2d 1303.

the environment."[147] Therefore, a "release" only occurs "whenever a hazardous substance is released from a facility, such as a tank or a lagoon, into the environment, such as the ground or the air."[148] As such, the EPA's interpretation of CERCLA's reporting requirement could not be reconciled with CERCLA's express terms, because "[r]ather than defining a release as the movement of a substance from a facility into the environment (as does CERCLA), the EPA defines a release as the placement of a substance into a facility that is exposed to the environment."[149]

Thus, because the term "environment" has a different meaning than the term "facility," where you can demonstrate that the client's waste contains background levels of trace inorganic hazardous substances (e.g., metals) that will not release any additional hazardous substances and that will also not migrate beyond the facility's boundaries into the subsurface or groundwater or air at or around the site, it would defy reason for a disposal at the "facility" alone—a disposal which has no possibility of migrating beyond the facility itself onto offsite adjacent land or into the air or groundwater—to be considered a release or threatened release into the "environment." If the attorney and consultant can gather the evidence to prove that the client's waste has none of these capabilities, they may be able to demonstrate that there has been no release of the client's waste into the environment beyond the facility that could trigger liability under CERCLA.

It should be noted that this is a difficult defense to mount, and it is unlikely that the necessary evidence will be available within the time frame required to file a motion to dismiss. Nonetheless, if the client's waste has been clearly delineated, and the site has been well characterized, it may be possible to bring an early motion for summary judgment on this issue.

---

147. Id. at 1309.

148. Ibid.

149. Ibid., emphasis in original.

5. CERCLA Requires That the Alleged Release or Threatened Release of Any Purportedly Hazardous Substance(s) from the PRP's Waste Must Cause the Incurrence of Response Costs

CERCLA requires that there be some connection between the alleged release or threatened release and the response costs incurred to remediate the environmental problems caused by the purported release or threatened release. CERCLA § 107 specifically requires that the defendant arrange for the disposal of hazardous substances at a facility where "a release, or a threatened release [occurs] . . . which causes the incurrence of response costs."[150] The "causation" issue was addressed by the Western District of Washington, which stated:

> There is a distinction between "causing a release" and "causing response costs." In other words, liability does not attach because the defendant caused "a release," but because it caused "response costs." While defendant may often cause both, it is the causing of response costs that subjects a party to liability under CERCLA. 42 U.S.C. § 9607(a)(3) and (4).[151]

If, for example, it can be argued that the alleged hazardous substances purportedly present in the PRP's waste are not leachable and cannot, even when added to other hazardous substances, have caused or contributed to the release of hazardous substances into the environment from the facility at the site in question, it should be clear that the PRP has not caused plaintiff to incur any of the response costs at issue. If your client has not caused the incurrence of any response costs at the subject site, they should not be subject to liability under CERCLA.[152]

In *Alcan I*, Alcan, a manufacturer of aluminum sheet and plate products, disposed of used emulsion into an air shaft or bore hole which in turn emptied into the Susquehanna River in Pittston, Pennsylvania. The emulsion contained low levels of metallic compounds. In November 1989, the government filed a complaint against twenty defendants, all of

---

150. CERCLA § 107(a)(4), 42 U.S.C. § 9607(a)(4).

151. *Louisiana-Pacific Corporation v. Asarco, Inc.* (W.D. Wash. 1990) 735 F.Supp. 358, 362 (*Louisiana-Pacific*); see also *Amoco Oil Co. v. Borden, Inc.* (5th Cir. 1989) 889 F.2d 664, 670-671.

152. See *United States v. Alcan Aluminum Corporation* (3d Cir. 1992) 964 F.2d 252, 271 (*Alcan I*).

whom settled except for Alcan, and then moved for summary judgment against Alcan to collect the balance of response costs due to the release of hazardous substances into the river. Alcan cross-moved for summary judgment, contending that its emulsion did not constitute a hazardous substance as defined by CERCLA and that its emulsion could not have caused the release or any response costs incurred by the government.

In *US v. Alcan Aluminum Corp.* (2nd Cir. 1993) 990 F.2d 711 (*Alcan II*), Alcan was once again the lone holdout in a case in which the government entered into a consent decree with eighty-two defendants covering 74% or $9,100,000 of cleanup costs incurred at a waste disposal and treatment center in Oswego County, New York. Once again, after the federal government and New York State moved for summary judgment, Alcan cross-moved for summary judgment, alleging, in addition to the hazardous substance issue, that causation had to be demonstrated under CERCLA and that the harm caused by Alcan's waste was divisible such that the government claim improperly subjected Alcan to joint and several liability. In both *Alcan I* and *Alcan II*, the appellate courts held that:

> Alcan may escape any liability for response costs if it either succeeds in proving that its oil emulsion, when mixed with other hazardous waste, did not contribute to the release and the cleanup costs that followed, or contributed at most to only a divisible portion of the harm.[153]

In *Alcan II*, the Second Circuit Court of Appeals stated that to avoid the harsh result which would follow if the scope of CERCLA liability had no limitation, it would allow the "causation" defense to be "reintroduced" at the apportionment stage of a CERCLA action where a defendant's waste contains minimal amounts of hazardous substances. Reintroducing "causation" would "permit a defendant to escape payment where its pollutants did not contribute more than background contamination and also cannot concentrate." (*Alcan II*, *supra*, 990 F.2d at 722.) Where a defendant can show that its alleged pollutants did not contribute more than background contamination and also cannot concentrate, the complete divisibility rule may exonerate the defendant from any liability under CERCLA. In *Louisiana-Pacific*, a third-party defendant USGI—a manufacturer of mineral wool used as insulation—produced a hazardous byproduct called "shot" in the manufacturing process. The USGI plant in Tacoma, Washington discarded approximately 7,000 cubic yards of shot at a landfill that was designated by the state of Washington as a site requiring cleanup.

---

153. *Alcan II*, supra, 990 F.2d at 722.

USGI argued that the real problem at the site was caused by slag deposited by the defendant Asarco in the landfill and by wood waste contributed by plaintiff Louisiana-Pacific. Although the US District Court for the Western District of Washington determined that USGI's shot was a hazardous substance under CERCLA, and that a release had occurred at the landfill, it did acknowledge that "CERCLA, however, does appear to provide a threshold for liability when it comes to 'cause.'"[154] The *Louisiana-Pacific* court went on to further explore the statutory requirement set forth in § 107 that the release of a hazardous substance at a facility must cause the incurrence of response costs, analyzing *Amoco Oil v. Borden* (5th Cir. 1989) 889 F.2d 664:

> The Amoco court addressed quantification and expressly rejected the notion that liability attaches upon the release of any specific quantity of hazardous substance. The court did so because otherwise it "would permit CERCLA's reach to exceed its statutory purposes by holding parties liable who have not posed any threat to the public or environment."[155]

As noted by the *Louisiana-Pacific* court, "the relevant factual inquiry . . . should focus on whether 'a hazardous substance that is deposited by a PRP' justified a response action."[156] Summary judgment was denied to USGI because third-party plaintiff Asarco had offered evidence that the shot USGI deposited at the landfill "may threaten a release that is likely to violate an applicable state or federal standard and thereby cause the incurrence of response costs."

Therefore, you may be able to escape liability in situations in which you and your environmental consultant can demonstrate that there are no hazardous substances in excess of known background soil levels, or that would leach out from your client's waste at the site, and there has been no release of any hazardous substances from your client's waste from the facility into the environment. You will need to show that the waste deposited by your client at the facility has neither caused nor threatened any release that is likely to violate any applicable state or federal standard, and as such, no response costs have been incurred by any regulatory agency or plaintiff(s) as a result of the depositing of your

154. *Louisiana-Pacific*, supra, 735 F.Supp. at 362

155. *Louisiana-Pacific*, supra, 735 F.Supp. at 362.

156. Ibid.

client's waste at the facility.

If you can assemble facts of this nature, you should consider answering the complaint and bringing an early motion for summary judgment on the grounds that your client has not caused the incurrence response costs as required by CERCLA § 107(a)(3), 42 U.S.C. § 9607(a)(3).

C. The Public Nuisance Defense

Sometimes, where the allegations in a complaint of the various levels of contamination caused by the activities or operations of a defendant are specific, it may be possible to file a demurrer or motion to dismiss on the grounds that the property's extremely low levels of soil and non-existent groundwater contamination have never presented a danger or risk to public health or the environment that would constitute an actionable public nuisance.

California Civil Code § 3480 defines a public nuisance as "one which affects at the same time an entire community or neighborhood, or any considerable number of persons, although the extent of the annoyance or damage inflicted upon individuals may be unequal." The focus in determining whether something is a public nuisance "must be upon whether an entire neighborhood or community or at least a considerable number of persons are affected in the manner and by the factors that make the thing a nuisance under Civil Code § 3479."[157] A public nuisance concerns "a situation that is injurious to public health, or is indecent or offensive to the senses of the public, or which is an obstruction to the free use of property by the public."[158]

The public nuisance in a soil and groundwater contamination case typically involves health concerns arising from dermal or inhalation exposure to contaminants in soil, or exposure to the same contaminants through the water supply (should the substances infiltrate the water supply). It may be possible to demonstrate on a threshold level that the contamination at issue does not pose a public nuisance where neither the allegations in the complaint, nor the various remedial investigation reports attached as exhibits to the complaint, contain any data that reveal injurious exposure to public health through soil or water.

If you can succeed in convincing the court that the contamination at issue in the

157. *Beck Development Co., Inc. v. Southern Pacific Transportation Co.* (1996) 44 Cal.App.4th 1160 (*Beck*).

158. Ibid.

action does not rise to the level of a public nuisance, you will have taken a significant step in eviscerating the viability of any other claims which remain in the complaint. In other words, all the plaintiff 's damages will be called into question.

In most situations, the public nuisance argument has two prongs: (1) that the types of contaminants and levels of contamination in the site soil do not present and have never presented a public health danger; and (2) that there is not and has never been any groundwater pathway for potential public exposure at the site in question. On the first prong, the complaint's allegations must demonstrate that none of the existing contamination or contamination that the plaintiff has remediated at the site presents or ever presented a threat or possibility of exposure to the contaminants (typically gasoline, motor oil, or diesel fuel) underlying the ground surface. In other words, you must argue that the substances beneath the land would have posed no risk to the health of any persons through the pathway of personal proximity if the alleged contaminants had been left where they were without any purported "remedial" action.

As to the second prong of the argument, the allegations of the complaint, as supported by laboratory data, must reveal no evidence of any groundwater contamination to drinking water (i.e., beneficial) aquifers, and no evidence that the alleged contamination under the subject property has migrated onto other properties or into the water supplies of other persons. If these facts can be shown, it should be indisputable that a groundwater pathway does not exist for potential exposure to the public at the site; it should also be indisputable that future contamination to groundwater or water supplies is unlikely. Therefore, a demurrer or motion to dismiss may be granted if the contaminants in the site soil do not present a public health danger, and there is no groundwater pathway for potential public exposure, because a public nuisance does not exist at the site.

Finally, it should also be noted that where a well-founded basis for a fear of future injury does not exist, the nuisance claim is speculative and without merit.[159]

159. *Payne v. McKinley* (1980) 54 Cal. 532, 533; *Koll-Irvine Center Property Owners Assn. v. County of Orange* (1994) 24 Cal.App.4th 1036, 1040-1041.

CASE STUDY 9:
Is a Land Use Covenant the End of the World?

Okay, it's time to get into the weeds. Like Sisyphus pushing that huge boulder up the hill forever, you might almost be done—after years of performing one investigation after another and cleaning up the site repeatedly using various arcane technologies as they came along. The regulator is poised to grant closure to your client and issue a No Further Action (NFA) letter, so long as the client will agree to execute and file a Land Use Covenant (LUC) with the County Recorder's office, which will run with the land and limit the uses of the property to commercial and industrial forever.

"What!" says the client. "I thought I was done. Everybody around me is tearing down their dilapidated buildings and erecting beautiful mixed-used developments that include apartments, healthcare facilities, and other sensitive uses. I cleaned up my property. Why can't I do the same?"

Well, there is a way. If you have development plans for the property, you can share the plans with the regulator. Attempt to calmly explain that all the residual contamination, which is located around the foundations of the old building onsite (which will soon be demolished) will be history, since more than 30 feet of soil will be removed to put in the 3 levels of subterranean parking for the new building. As such, not a trace of the old contamination will be left.

How can this not placate the regulator? Let us count the ways. First, the regulator may have concerns about the residual contaminated soil which will be stockpiled onsite before it is disposed of at a landfill. Will it be characterized as hazardous or nonhazardous waste? What about the worker safety issues for the contractors and construction crews that will be working onsite around the stockpiles? Is there a soils management plan to address these various issues?

Next, what about the relatively shallow groundwater beneath the site that will remain contaminated with VOCs either slightly below or slightly above the MCLs? It's a pain, to be sure. Welcome, Plan B. Plan B offers a compromise in the context of the acknowledged limitations of the LUC. Plan B says:

- Covenantor promises to restrict the use of the Burdened Property as follows:

  a. Development and use of the Premises located on the Burdened Property shall be restricted primarily to industrial, commercial, and/or office space.

  b. No residence for human habitation shall be permitted on the first floor of the slab-on-grade structure located upon or in the vicinity of the Premises located on the Burdened Property.

  c. No hospitals shall be permitted on the Burdened Property.

  d. No public or private schools for persons under 21 years of age shall be permitted on the first floor of the slab-on-grade structures of the Burdened Property.

  e. In lieu of modifying or removing any improvements, the Owner may choose to implement further cleanup or abatement of subsurface contaminants under Board oversight, to the point where the health risk posed by those contaminants is reduced to meet unrestricted land use standards.

  f. No Owner or Occupant shall drill, bore, otherwise construct, or use a well for the purpose of extracting water for domestic, potable, or industrial uses, unless expressly permitted in writing by the Board; nor shall the Owner or Occupant permit or engage any third party to do such acts.

g. The Covenantor agrees that the Board, and any persons acting pursuant to Board orders, shall have reasonable access to the Burdened Property for the purposes of inspection, surveillance, maintenance, or monitoring, as provided in Division 7 of the Water Code.

We have used this exact language in several LUCs with various state agencies. It's logical and it works. The compromise is that no ultra-sensitive uses such as hospitals are allowed. However, the LUC contemplates that schools or residences can be in newly designed and constructed developments, as long they are not on the first floor. Why? Because, to the extent that a vapor intrusion risk remains, it is unlikely to extend beyond the first floor.

It's not a home run, but it will enable the client to basically do what he wants with his property.

D. Ability to Pay (ATP) Defense to State or Federal Liability

California has established basic protocols for determining whether a party claiming financial prejudice should be excused from paying response costs incurred by the state in the investigation and cleanup of contaminated properties.[160]

If you want more specifics than we have the room or inclination to provide here, take a look at the November 21, 2013 Departmental Procedures Memorandum issued by

160. See Cal. Health & Saf. Code §§ 25187(b)(1)(B), 25360 et seq., and 25390 et seq.

the California Department of Toxic Substances Control (DTSC), entitled "Cost Recovery: Ability to Pay (ATP) Determinations." The DTSC policy is modeled after the EPA's "General Policy on Superfund Ability to Pay Determinations" (Sept. 1997).

Let's start with a basic scenario. You represent a small dry cleaner owner/operator who has been operating a dry-cleaning facility on family-owned property in a depressed neighborhood for a period of 30 to 40 years. A public school was recently built on property adjacent to your client's property. In the course of acquiring the school property by eminent domain and commissioning various environmental impact studies, it was discovered that soil vapor contamination from the dry-cleaning site had migrated onto the school property. Your client has limited financial resources and insufficient insurance to pay for the significant investigation, cleanup costs, and regulatory oversight fees, which have been going through the roof as the matter drags out for a period of nearly 10 years.

What do you do? You tell the DTSC that your client is on the verge of financial collapse.

What does DTSC do? Here's a glimpse of what happens, taken directly from the DTSC policy memo on ATP Claims:

> *The Ability to Pay (ATP) Analysis*
> 1. When a Department employee is contacted by a billable party that claims an inability to pay the Department's response costs, the employee will immediately notify the Project Manager for the site regarding the billable party's claim.
> a. The Project Manager or Branch Liaison will prepare a letter to the billable party requesting financial information necessary to evaluate the billable party's inability to pay claim.
> i. The type of information requested from the billable party will depend on whether the billable party claiming an inability to pay is an individual or a corporation/business entity.
> b. If the billable party is a corporation or business entity, then the Department requires the following financial information to conduct the ATP analysis:
> i. Federal and state income tax returns for the last three years, including all schedules, exhibits, and attachments.
> ii. Financial statements for the last three years (the same

period of time).

iii. The current financial statement.

iv. The most recent 12 months of bank statements for any and all checking, savings, lines of credit, and investment accounts.

c. If the billable party is an individual, then the Department requires the following financial information to conduct the ATP analysis:

i. Federal and state income tax returns for the last three years, including all schedules, exhibits, and attachments.

ii. A current financial statement using the sample financial statement format, which is available on the Cost Recovery Policies and Procedures SharePoint page at http://dtscshare/PP/CostRecovery/default.aspx.

iii. The most recent 12 months of bank statements for any and all checking, savings, credit cards, loans, lines of credit, and investment accounts.

The process seems simple enough until your client thinks about actually doing these things. Bottom line: *You must lay yourself bare.*

If the billable party provides the requested financial information or documentation, the project manager will enter the financial information obtained into one of the EPA's enforcement economic models. EPA models analyze the financial aspects of a responsible party's ability to pay for enforcement actions, compliance costs, cleanup costs, and/or civil penalties. The models are modified annually as part of the EPA's routine update process. Updates to the models include financial information (i.e., current tax rates, inflation rates, discount/compound rates) and utility enhancement. The relevant models are: 1) ABEL, which evaluates a corporation's or partnership's ability to pay; and 2) INDIPAY, which evaluates an individual's ability to pay. The models are available at http://www2.epa.gov/enforcement/penalty-and-financial-models.

The billable party's financial information will be kept confidential.

This is heady stuff, but extremely important and rewarding to your client if they are really in a financial crisis. Not only can a successful ATP outcome relieve the client from paying past regulatory response costs, but future costs can also be excused. Further, if the client actually owns the contaminated property and wants to save it (in terms of restoring its value), showing an inability to pay is a prerequisite for qualifying for such grant programs as the Site Cleanup Subaccount Program (SCAP), sponsored by the California State Water

Resources Control Board (the "State Water Board," or "SWRCB", parent agency of the nine Regional Water Quality Control Boards) and to the substantial grant money that has recently become available to DTSC through SB 158, the $500 million hazardous waste bill signed into law in 2021 by Governor Gavin Newsom. The bill allocated $500 million to expedite the cleanup and beneficial reuse of idled contaminated properties in historically vulnerable and disadvantaged communities.

The SCAP program implemented by the State Water Board and Regional Water Boards is a non-competitive funding program established by California Health & Safety Code Section 25299.6 in 2014. It allows the State Water Board to issue grants for reasonable and necessary costs associated with projects that remediate the harm or threat of harm to human health, safety, or the environment caused by existing or threatened surface or groundwater contamination. More information on this and other funding programs is available at: www.waterboards.ca.gov/water_issues/programs/grants_loans/.

How does one navigate these treacherous waters in terms of preparing financial statements, balance sheets, running data through complex computer models, and responding to sophisticated staffers at DTSC or the State Water Board who want answers to many questions? You need a good forensic accountant to guide you through the process.

Light At the End of The Tunnel

If you've read our section above on the Ability to Pay defense to state or federal liability, you're already familiar with the following basic scenario. You represent a small business owner who has been operating a dry-cleaning facility on family-owned property in a depressed neighborhood for a period of 30 to 40 years. A public school was recently built on property adjacent to your client's property. In the course of acquiring the school property by eminent domain and commissioning various environmental impact studies, the school district discovered that soil vapor contamination from the dry-cleaning site had migrated onto the school property. Your client has limited financial resources and insufficient insurance to pay for the significant investigation, cleanup costs, litigation costs, and regulatory oversight fees which have been going through the roof as the matter drags on for a period of nearly 10 years.

What do you do? You tell the school district that's suing your client and the California Department of Toxic Substances Control (DTSC) that is overseeing the site investigations at the school and at the dry cleaner's property that your client is on the verge of financial collapse.

What does DTSC do? It says: "prove it." In our ATP section, we explained that the ATP process will require your client to lay himself bare in terms of the financial information. Ultimately, the school district isn't interested in a worthless, uncollectable judgment. If DTSC will take over the cleanup, or help your client qualify for a funding grant to finish the cleanup, that's all that matters.

As explained in our ATP section, if the client qualifies under the ATP process, he can apply to the Site Cleanup Subaccount Program (SCAP) sponsored by the California State Water Resources Control Board ("State Water Board"), the parent agency of the nine Regional Water Quality Control Boards. Or he can apply for a similar grant administered by DTSC.

Further, if there's a recalcitrant insurer that doesn't want to pay for anything, and the regulator is willing to accept that your client is destitute with the exception of limited insurance, the DTSC or the State Water Board may relieve the respondent of any further liability in order to prompt the respondent's insurer to cash out its coverage. The dry cleaning operator's insurer can pay the limits of all remaining coverage and exhaust the policy as long as the insured faces no further liability as memorialized in a judicial consent decree, which would include contribution protection from suits by anybody else and would also contain a covenant not to ever sue the insured in the future.

E. CLRRA Immunity

The California Land Reuse and Revitalization Act of 2004 (hereinafter "CLRRA") was enacted by Assembly Bill No. 389, Montanez, on September 23, 2004, to encourage and establish the cleanup and reuse of underused urban properties that would otherwise be subject to liability from historic contamination, in a manner that is protective of public health and safety and the environment. CLRRA provides for an eligible bona fide purchaser ("BFP"), innocent landowner ("ILO"), or contiguous property owner ("CPO") to qualify for specified immunities from liability for certain response costs or damage claims under applicable state statutes.

Under CLRRA, a prospective purchaser, innocent owner, or the owner of an adjacent property may enter into an agreement with the California Department of Toxic Substances Control or one of the California Regional Water Quality Control Boards for carrying out the necessary evaluation and remediation of a contaminated and underutilized urban site. The agreement requires the person to perform various actions, including conducting a site assessment and, if necessary, preparing and implementing a response plan. Once the terms of the agreement have been fulfilled, the person will be afforded limited immunity from further liability for the contamination. This immunity can then be passed on to future owners, users, and lenders, which greatly enhances the opportunities for redevelopment or reuse of the affected property. The CLRRA program is a voluntary program afforded to qualifying BFPs, CPOs, or ILOs, and does not alter existing state law regarding liability for releases or discharges of hazardous substances or hazardous materials not addressed by this Agreement.

To participate, the property and owner must meet all the following criteria:

- The owner cannot be responsible for the contamination.
- The property must be located in an urban infill area—a vacant or underutilized property in a populated area.
- The property cannot be part of a state or federal listed superfund site.
- The property cannot be an underground storage tank (UST) site impacted by petroleum.

Some of the highlights of this act are as follows:

- Participants agree to assess and clean up the property as necessary.
- Participants seeking to qualify for immunity must enter into an agreement with an oversight agency.
- Immunities begin at the time the agreement is signed.
- Response actions must be as protective of public health, safety, and the environment as actions required under Health and Safety Code, Division 20, Chapter 6.8 and Division 7 of the Water Code.
- Specific public participation requirements apply.
- Future property owners may also qualify for immunity provided they meet all of the qualifying conditions and they comply with the terms of the agreement.
- Chapter 6.82 currently has a sunset date of January 1, 2027 (unless it is renewed, as it most recently was in 2016), but any immunities will continue after that date.
- A bona fide purchaser may consult with an oversight agency to facilitate the purchaser's decision to apply to the program.

Pursuant to Section 25395.81 of the California Health & Safety Code, the bona fide purchaser, innocent landowner, or contiguous property owner is "not liable under any applicable statute for a claim made by any person, other than an agency, for response costs or other damages associated with a release or threatened release of a hazardous material at the site characterized in the site assessment conducted pursuant to, or a response plan approved pursuant to, Article 6 (commencing with Section 25395.90)."

In other words, if the eligible applicant performs under the CLRRA agreement with the regulator, the applicant is protected from third-party liability to any other entities or persons who may own or operate other properties in the vicinity (or who owned or operated said properties in the past) and who may allege that the eligible participant contaminated their properties.

A CLRRA Agreement can have some flexibility. For instance, in a situation where our client was purchasing contaminated property, the deal with the seller was contingent on the buyer's CLRRA application being accepted and, critically, with the seller agreeing to be the work party performing the investigation and cleanup work. We were able to make the deal work because the Los Angeles Regional Water Quality Control Board accepted our client's CLRRA application.

F. Motion to Strike Punitive Damage Claims

Relaxed and general pleading is not allowed in the punitive damage arena. Here, "vague, conclusory allegations of fraud or falsity may not be rescued by the rule of liberal construction."[161] Further, where a negligent or "non-deliberate injury is charged, allegations that the defendants' conduct was wrongful, willful, wanton, reckless, or unlawful do not support a claim for exemplary damages; such allegations do not charge malice."[162] Where the thrust of the action is negligence, and the plaintiff has done nothing but allege boilerplate conclusory facts praying for a punitive damage recovery, grounds may exist to file a motion to strike the complaint's claims for punitive damage.

Civil Code Section 3294 contains the following definitions:

1. "Malice" means conduct which is intended by the defendant to cause injury to the plaintiff or despicable conduct which is carried on by the defendant with a willful and conscious disregard of the rights or safety of others.
2. "Oppression" means despicable conduct that subjects a person to cruel and unjust hardship in conscious disregard of that person's rights.

"Despicable conduct" is defined as "conduct which is so vile, base, or contemptible that it would be looked down upon and despised by reasonable people."[163]

A motion to strike should be granted unless specific facts are alleged to support the punitive damage claim.[164] *Grieves v. Superior Court* dealt with charges that a physician had engaged in negligent and intentional conduct leading to commission of a surgery without

---

161. *G.D. Searle & Co. v. Superior Court* (1975) 49 Cal.App.3d 22, 30

162. Ibid.

163. CACI No. 3941, (2020 Rev.). BAJI No. 14.72.1 defines "despicable conduct" much the same way, as "conduct which is so vile, base, contemptible, miserable, wretched, or loathsome that it would be looked down upon and despised by *ordinary decent people*" (emphasis added). Note that BAJI is no longer officially approved by state court rules, having been supplanted by CACI. See California Judicial Council, Civil Jury Instructions FAQ, https://www.courts.ca.gov/partners/315.htm.

164. *Grieves v. Superior Court* (1984) 157 Cal.App.3d 159, 164.

consent. The complaint contained allegations that the conduct of the doctor was "willful, malicious, fraudulent, and oppressive." Nevertheless, the trial court granted defendant's motion to strike, and this decision was affirmed on appeal. The Court of Appeal found that the operative facts in the complaint failed to show precisely why that conduct could be considered sufficient to give rise to punitive damages, stating:

> The mere allegation an intentional tort was committed is not sufficient to warrant an award of punitive damages. Not only must there be circumstances of oppression, fraud, or malice, but facts must be alleged in the pleading to support such a claim.[165]

Likewise, in your case, grounds may exist to strike the punitive damage allegations from the complaint. This is possible where the plaintiff does not allege any egregious conduct with respect to any of the negligence-based causes of action indicating anything other than that the client has purportedly contaminated the property at issue in the complaint by using and occupying the property over a period of years, and no specific incidents or particular conduct is alleged.

As to punitive damage allegations attached to claims of fraud and intentional or negligent misrepresentation, if the plaintiff alleges no specific facts justifying punitive damages for these claims, and the conclusory allegations seeking punitive damages are unsupported by specific facts in the pleading, the allegations will be construed as ambiguous, and an argument can be made that they should be disregarded.[166]

G. Counterclaims, Cross-Claims, Third-Party Complaints, and Cross-Complaints

The answer to the complaint should not be taken lightly. A diligent environmental counsel must carefully set forth all affirmative defenses necessary to avoid liability under plaintiff's complaint, and in federal court (or in the case of a verified complaint in state court) prepare specific denials on a paragraph-by-paragraph basis. However, the answer is merely

165. Id. at 166.

166. See *Interior Systems, Inc. v. Del E. Webb, Corp.* (1981) 122 Cal.App.3d 312, 316.

a starting point. There are two critical issues which counsel must confront before the answer is due: which further offensive pleading should be filed, and whether any additional parties should be named.

1. Contribution

It should preliminarily be assumed in a CERCLA action that any defendant who has been sued will have a contribution claim under CERCLA § 113(f), 42 U.S.C. § 9613(f). That section permits any party named in a CERCLA § 107 action to seek contribution from other potentially liable parties during or following any action under CERCLA §§ 106 or 107. It should be noted, however, that where PRP defendants settle out of a case, the non-settling defendant's (i.e., your) right to demand contribution from them will be extinguished by the settlement. Nonetheless, settling PRPs who are parties to a CERCLA settlement retain the right to seek contribution from non-settling PRPs, pursuant to 42 U.S.C. § 9613(f)(3)(B).

Most federal courts have held that there is no right to a jury trial for contribution actions under CERCLA § 113. The court, in a § 113 action, "may allocate response costs among liable parties using such equitable factors as the court determines are appropriate."[167] In other words, after determining which parties are liable under § 107, the court will apportion liability among the parties using whatever factors it deems necessary to achieve a just and equitable allocation among the parties.[168]

There are no hard and fast rules concerning the factors the court will consider when deciding whether or how to grant apportionment. The congressional factors, often called the "Gore factors" (after then-US representative Al Gore), and set forth in the act's legislative history, proposed that the following considerations be made in allocating liability:

1. The ability of each PRP to demonstrate that its contribution to a discharge, release, or disposal of a hazardous waste can be distinguished.
2. The amount or quantity of each PRP's hazardous waste.
3. The degree of toxicity of materials each PRP is responsible

167. 42 U.S.C. § 9613(f)(1).

168. See *United States v. R.W. Meyer, Inc.* (6th Cir. 1991) 932 F.2d 568, 572.

for releasing or discharging at the facility in question.
4. The degree of involvement of each PRP in the generation, transportation, treatment, storage, or disposal of the hazardous waste in question.
5. The degree of care exercised by each PRP with respect to the hazardous waste involved.
6. The degree of cooperation of each PRP with relevant government officials to prevent any harm to public health or the environment.

The Gore factors were contained in an amendment that was passed by the House but that was not ultimately incorporated into the Act. Nonetheless, they are routinely used by most courts as tools to facilitate the allocation of contribution claims.

Additional factors authorized by CERCLA § 122(e), 42 U.S.C. § 9622(e) include

1. the mobility (and/or migratory potential) of the hazardous substances involved,
2. the strength of evidence pertaining to the PRP's involvement at the site,
3. the PRP's ability to pay,
4. litigation risks inherent in dealing with the PRP, and
5. public interest considerations.

In CERCLA litigation, the four categories of responsible parties are set forth in the statute, 42 U.S.C. § 9607(a). They are:

1. Past and present property owners[169]
2. Past and present operators (e.g., lessees) of the property or facility where the hazardous release occurred[170]
3. Transporters who selected the site for disposal or treatment of hazardous substances[171]

---

169. 42 U.S.C. § 9607(a)(1), (2).

170. Ibid.

171. 42 U.S.C. § 9607(a)(4).

4. Arrangers for disposal[172]

Although many courts have failed to make clear distinctions between the terms "owner" and "operator" in the CERCLA context, it should be noted that under CERCLA, the concept of liability is all-encompassing as to owners. For liability to attach, the PRP needs either to have owned the facility in question at the time the hazardous releases occurred or to have acquired the property after the hazardous releases occurred without performing the due diligence required to be entitled to the safe harbor of the "innocent landowner" defense.

The analysis, however, should be slightly more rigorous for the determination of whether *operator* liability attaches. As the Ninth Circuit has reasoned, "to be an operator of a hazardous waste facility, a party must do more than stand by and fail to prevent the contamination. It must play an active role in running the facility, typically involving hands-on, day-to-day participation in the facility's management."[173]

The court may consider the following elements in determining whether an individual qualifies as an operator:

- Whether the individual can control work at the plant
- Whether the individual can choose or has chosen employees
- Whether the individual directs employee activities
- Whether the individual sets prices[174]

Just as the plaintiff must consider whether the named PRPs qualify as owners or operators under CERCLA, the defendant, in considering counterclaims, cross-claims, or third-party complaints, should also consider whether the basic thresholds discussed above have been met. If counsel is answering a RCRA complaint or claim, consideration should be given to whether there is any "past or present owner or operator of [the] storage or disposal facility" who has not been named by the plaintiff in the suit brought against the client.[175]

---

172. 42 U.S.C. § 9607(a).

173. *Long Beach Unified School District v. Godwin Liv. Trust* (9th Cir. 1994) 32 F.3d 1364, 1367.

174. See *Edward Hines Lumber Co. v. Vulvan Materials Co.* (7th Cir. 1988) 861 F.2d 155, 157-58.

175. 42 U.S.C. § 6972(a)(1)(B).

CERCLA basically ignores the traditional rules and niceties of corporate liability and imposes direct owner or operator liability on shareholders, officers, or directors of a corporation if the corporation itself is liable as an owner or operator under CERCLA. The majority of courts that have ignored the corporate formalities to impose personal liability for corporate acts have reasoned that CERCLA allows for the imposition of personal liability where the director, officer, or shareholder had the authority to control operations at the facility or had the authority to prevent the contamination by his corporation.[176] Similarly, it has been argued that under CERCLA, a parent corporation may have liability as an owner or operator where the parent has the ability to control the environmental acts of the subsidiary.[177]

The Supreme Court, however, has ruled that a parent corporation may be held directly liable as an operator only where it actively participated in and exercised control over a subsidiary's business during a period of hazardous waste disposal.[178] Thus, all predecessors and successors-in-interest in corporate lineage, including shareholders of dissolved corporations, should be investigated. In addition, all predecessors and successors-in-interest on title for the contaminated site in question should be investigated as potential third-party defendants, including general and limited partners to real estate syndicates connected with the contamination problem. Chemical suppliers and manufacturers, equipment suppliers and manufacturers, architects and designers of manufacturing plants should all be investigated as potential third-party defendants.

In addition to the potential third-party defendants, if appropriate under extreme circumstances, environmental counsel may consider whether plaintiff's own environmental consultant should be named as a party when considering either a potential CERCLA claim or a state law indemnity claim, and whether any potential municipality defendants exist who created a dangerous condition or contributed to the spreading of contamination at the site.

---

176. See *Donahey v. Bogle* (6th Cir. 1993) 987 F.2d 1250 [applying "prevention test"]; *City of North Miami, Florida v. Berger* (E.D. Va. 1993) 828 F.Supp. 401 [applying "authority to control" standard].

177. See *United States v. Kayser-Roth* (1st Cir. 1990) 910 F.2d 24.

178. *US v. Best Foods* (1998) 524 U.S. 51, 53, 118 S.Ct. 1876, 1881.

2. Inverse Condemnation

In addition to the obvious nuisance and trespass claims which may be asserted in the factual scenario described above, you can also assert an inverse condemnation claim against governmental entities. Article I, § 19 of the California Constitution mandates that "private property may be taken or damaged for public use only when just compensation, ascertained by a jury unless waived, has first been paid to or into court for the owner."

In addition to property owners, the inverse condemnation section may also be applied to a lessee. Lessees need only show that they own a property interest which has been taken by the public entity in order to be constitutionally entitled to compensation under an inverse condemnation theory.[179]

Inverse condemnation, unlike negligence, "does not require any breach of a standard of care, nor foreseeability of the harm."[180] In addition, it should be noted that although inverse condemnation actions typically involve damage to or a taking of real property, the remedy of inverse condemnation is also available for loss or damage to personal property.[181] To prevail in an inverse condemnation claim, apart from establishing an interest in the damaged property at the time of injury, the plaintiff or cross-complainant must also establish

- the defendant's planning, approval, construction, operation of, or substantial participation in an activity for public use or benefit;
- the defendant's taking or damaging of plaintiff 's property; and
- that the defendant's action was a proximate or substantial cause of the damage to the plaintiff's property.

The term "public use" refers to "a use which concerns the whole community or

---

179. *McMahan's v. City of Santa Monica* (1983) 146 Cal.App.3d 683, 690-91; *Aetna Life & Cas. Co. v. Los Angeles* (1985) 170 Cal.App.3d 865, 875.

180. *Aetna Life & Cas. Co. v. Los Angeles*, supra, 170 Cal.App.3d at 873.

181. *Eli v. State* (1975) 46 Cal.App.3d 233, 235.

promotes the general interest in its relation to any legitimate object of government."[182] The construction and maintenance of a landfill or waste disposal facility are certainly public uses that concern public policy.

Proximate cause can be established if the public improvement constitutes a substantial concurring cause; that is, if the injury occurred in substantial part because the improvement failed to function as it was intended.[183] For example, California courts have consistently held that the "construction and maintenance of storm drainage systems are matters of 'public policy,' and [that] such a system created by a public entity becomes a 'public improvement' and a 'public use.'"[184] Further, "drainage systems concern the whole community."[185]

Therefore, liability may be imposed on the public entity defendant if the plaintiff or cross-complainant can demonstrate that the public improvement, like a landfill or storm drain, "failed to function within its design capacity and thus constituted a substantial concurring—or a proximate—cause of the damages,"[186] even if the public entity was not negligent in its operation or maintenance of the improvement.

In addition to all damages due as just compensation for taken and/or damaged property, any party prevailing against a public entity on an inverse condemnation claim is also entitled to recover all reasonable costs, disbursements, and expenses, pursuant to California Code of Civil Procedure § 1036. This includes reasonable attorney, appraisal, and engineering fees incurred because of the proceeding. Interest on the judgment may also be assessed from the date of the taking, rather than from the date of judgment.[187]

---

182. *Frustuck v. City of Fairfax* (1963) 212 Cal.App.2d 345, 358.

183. *Belair v. Riverside City Flood Control Dist.* (1988) 47 Cal.3d 550, 559 (*Belair*).

184. *Marin v. City of San Rafael* (1980) 111 Cal.App.3d 591, 595.

185. *Frustuck v. City of Fairfax*, supra, 212 Cal.App.2d at 362.

186. *Belair*, supra, 47 Cal.3d at 562.

187. See *Youngblood v. Los Angeles County Flood Control Dist.* (1961) 56 Cal.2d 603, 611-12; *Ingram v. City of Redondo Beach* (1975) 45 Cal.App.3d 628 [Inverse condemnation liability should normally follow in a case in which the earth and retaining wall of a drainage sump collapsed, allowing flood waters to flow onto properties and inundate the plaintiffs' homes].

Glossary of Environmental Terms

Here is a glossary of environmental terms which will help you stay up-to-date with key environmental terms and jargon relating to environmental compliance, remediation, and sustainability.

#

100-year flood: also called the "base flood," this is a flood having a 1% chance of being equaled or exceeded in magnitude in a given year. It is *not* a flood occurring once every 100 years.

A

Aboveground Storage Tank (AST): frequently referred to as "bulk storage containers," these tanks and their piping and containment systems are used for storage of petroleum products.

Adsorbtion: the attachment of a substance to another, as oil might attach itself to grains of sand.

Advection: the transport of dissolved constituents with groundwater and is therefore dependent upon the hydraulic conductivity of the subsurface materials and hydraulic gradient in the aquifer.

Aerobic biodegradation: the breakdown of organic contaminants by micro-organisms into smaller organic compounds when oxygen is present; carbon dioxide and water are often the final products.

Air Knife: uses air and vacuum to carefully excavate up to six feet into the ground to pre-clear a hole, thus mitigating the risk of drilling into an expensive underground utility.

Air Permitting: major sources of air pollutants and certain other sources must obtain and operate in compliance with a Title V Permit–otherwise known as an operating permit under the Clean Air Act; sources are required to certify compliance annually, at the least.

Air Sparging: a technique for remediating contamination in **aquifers,** consisting of introducing air bubbles into the aquifer to volatilize the contaminants, allowing them to be removed by using **SVE.**

Air Toxics: chemicals released into the air that are known or suspected to cause cancer or other serious health problems.

Aliphatic Compounds: a group of organic chemical compounds in which the carbon atoms are linked in open chains or ring compounds with double bonds.

All-Appropriate Inquiry Rule (AAI Rule): provides an escape from liability called the "innocent landowner defense," but can only be used if appropriate due diligence was conducted prior to the acquisition of the property.

American Society of Testing and Materials (ASTM International): voluntary technical standards development organization that covers 15 industries and a wide range of products, systems, and services.

Anaerobic biodegradation: the breakdown of organic contaminants by micro-organisms when oxygen is not present.

Anaerobic Respiration: some anaerobic bacteria use nitrate, sulfate, iron, manganese, or carbon dioxide as their electron acceptors, and break down organic chemicals into smaller compounds, often producing carbon dioxide and methane as final products.

Analyte: compound for which an analytical laboratory has been requested to analyze a given sample or set of samples.

Anoxic: "without oxygen"; anoxic groundwater contains no dissolved oxygen which is a common situation at hazardous waste sites–biodegradation processes often use up all of the available oxygen.

Anthropogenic: caused by humans rather than nature.

AQMD: Air Quality Management District.

Aqueous Solubility: ability of a solution to be dissolved in water.

Aquiclude: a body of rock that will slowly absorb water but will not transmit the water fast enough to supply a well or spring (from Dictionary of Geological Terms).

Aquifer: pockets of water existing below the water table; underground layer of water-bearing permeable rock or unconsolidated materials (e.g., gravel, sand, silt, clay) capable of a sustainable yield of a significant amount of water to a well or spring.

Aquitard: body of impermeable or distinctly less-permeable material stratigraphically adjacent to one of more aquifers which slows but does not prevent the flow of water to or from an adjacent aquifer.

Aromatic Compounds: hydrocarbons containing one or more rings with double bonds (e.g., benzene).

Asbestos: naturally-occurring group of minerals that are found in the environment as bundles of durable fibers that are fire-, heat-, and chemical-resistant and do not conduct electricity; upon disturbance, fibers become airborne and can become trapped in the lungs upon inhalation.

B

Background contamination: the concentration of a regulated substance that is present at the site, but is not related to the release of a regulated substance at the site.

Best Management Practices (BMPs): practical and effective measures taken to protect natural resources; has referred to pollution controls in the fields of industrial wastewater control, stormwater management, and wetland management.

BFP: Bona Fide Purchaser. When referring to a prospective purchaser, the acronym "BFPP" can be used.

Biodegradation: breakdown of organic contaminants into smaller compounds by microbial organisms through metabolic or enzymatic processes, with carbon dioxide or methane as the final product; processes vary greatly but are key in the natural attenuation of contaminants of leaking underground storage tank and hazardous waste spill sites.

Brownfield: a formerly developed property that is about to be redeveloped, but the reconstruction process may be complicated by the presence of a hazardous substance or pollutant; often have high levels of subsurface contamination generated during operation.

BTEX: benzene, toluene, ethylbenzene, and xylene are four Volatile Organic Compounds found in gasoline; often found together and are similar in chemical properties; mobile in the subsurface and in the atmosphere, and of concern for underground storage tank remediation sites due to their mobility and toxicity.

C

CALTRANS: California Department of Transportation.

Capillary Fringe: mostly saturated (or completely saturated) zone just above the water table in which groundwater is drawn up from a water table; water content decreases with distance above the water table (pores at the base of the capillary fringe are fully saturated due to tension saturation; if pore size is small and relatively uniform, it is possible that soils can be completely saturated with water for several feet above the water table; if pore size is large, the saturated portion will extend only a few inches above the water table).

Carbon Monoxide (CO): a colorless, odorless, and tasteless gas that is produced by the incomplete combustion of fossil fuels and the burning of wood, propane, gas, charcoal, and other fuels; replaces oxygen in red blood cells, reducing oxygen supply to organs and tissues.

CERCLA: Comprehensive Environmental Response, Compensation, and Liability Act of 1980.

CFR: Code of Federal Regulations.

CIH: Certified Industrial Hygienist. The American Board of Industrial Hygiene (ABIH) provides qualified professionals with this certification.

CLRRA: the California Land Reuse and Revitalization Act of 2004, enacted to encourage and establish the cleanup and reuse of underused urban properties which might otherwise be subject to liability for historic contamination.

Co-metabolic/Co-metabolism: when two or more micro-organisms are required for the biodegradation of petroleum hydrocarbons; some compounds that are resistant to standard monocultural biodegradation have proved to be biodegradable with combinations of two, three, or more different species.

Commercial Energy Audit: determines the most effective low-cost means of reducing energy use by providing a breakdown of how, where, and when electricity is used at a business as well as potential engineering and financial modifications that may yield energy savings.

Commercial Property: refers to buildings or lands intended to generate a profit either from capital gain or rental income.

Comprehensive General Liability (CGL) Insurance: Comprehensive general liability (CGL) insurance is a type of insurance policy that provides defense and indemnity to an insured business or person against third party losses (that is, losses suffered by businesses or persons other than the insured to whom the insured may be legally responsible) for property damage, bodily injury, personal injury, and advertising injury claims.

Comprehensive Phase II Environmental Site Assessment: includes extensive sampling to fully characterize the extent of contamination as well as analyses of potential migration.

Confined Aquifer: an aquifer separated from the ground surface or overlying aquifer by an aquiclude or aquitard to the extent that pressure can be created in the lower reaches of the aquifer without affecting either the soil surface or the upper reservoir of water.

Constituents of Concern (COCs): contaminants in environmental media that may cause a risk to human health, safety, or the environment that have been identified for further evaluation, such as risk assessment.

Contaminant: regulated substance released into the environment.

CPO: Contiguous Property Owner.

Corrective Action Plan: document describing exactly–often step-by-step–how a specific situation will be changed to achieve a targeted outcome.

D

Data Quality Objectives (DQOs): qualitative and quantitative statements specified to ensure that data of known and appropriate quality are obtained; involves a logical step-by-step procedure for determining which of the complex issues affecting a site are the most relevant to planning a site investigation before any data are collected.

Dense Non-Aqueous Phase Liquid (DNAPL): "pure product" (e.g., dry cleaning fluid) that remains undiluted as the original bulk liquid in the subsurface; more dense than water and will sink when they reach the water table.

Diesel Fuel: another type of fuel oil which is denser than **gasoline** and, unlike gasoline, contains no **benzene.** It consists predominantly of hydrocarbon molecules in the range of C12 through C20.

Diffusion: spread of chemicals from areas of higher concentration to areas of lower concentration.

Dispersion: spread of dissolved constituents predominantly in the direction of groundwater flow, but also in directions other than would be expected due to groundwater movement only (lateral and vertical); causes some attenuation of the concentrations (lower concentrations) as the constituent move down-gradient.

DTSC: California's Department of Toxic Substances Control.

E

Effective Solubility: the maximum dissolved-phase concentration when a compound is part of a chemical mixture, calculated from the compound's mole fraction in the mixture and its pure-phase solubility in water; always less than the chemical's pure-phase solubility in water.

EIT: Engineer in Training. This is the first step under California toward becoming licensed as a professional engineer, but a person with an EIT certification is not yet a professional state-licensed engineer. An EIT only needs to have three or more years of study or experience, and may not even have their undergraduate degree yet.

Environmental Compliance: conforming to environmental laws, standards, and regulations to avoid future liability and to protect human health and the environment.

Environmental Media: soil, sediment, surface water, groundwater, bedrock, and air.

Environmental Professional: an individual who possesses sufficient education, training, and experience necessary to exercise professional judgment to develop opinions and conclusions regarding the presence or threat of releases to the surface or subsurface of a property.

Environmental Protection Agency: (EPA) Federal government agency created to protect human health and the environment through research, monitoring, standard-testing, and enforcement actions.

Environmentally-Sensitive Area: type of designation for an agricultural area which needs special protection of its landscape, wildlife, or historical value.

Equitable Tolling: a doctrine that can lengthen the time for bringing a lawsuit under certain conditions, such as when the plaintiff was prevented from bringing the lawsuit in some extraordinary way, or timely asserted their rights in the wrong forum.

F

Fermentation: takes place when the organic chemical acts as an electron acceptor.

Flammable Range: range of a concentration of a gas or vapor that will burn or explode if an ignition source is introduced; also known as "Explosive Range."

Flood Plain: any land area susceptible to being inundated by floodwaters. A 100-year flood plain refers to the area that would be expected be covered by water in the event of a **100-year flood.**

FOIA: the Freedom of Information Act, a federal statute allowing people to obtain records from the federal government.

FRCP: the Federal Rules of Civil Procedure, the procedural rules which govern lawsuits in federal courts. California has its own distinct rules, the California Code of Civil Procedure (CCP).

Free Product: regulated substance that is present as a separate phase liquid; liquid not dissolved in water.

G

Gasoline: typically composed of C4 to C12 hydrocarbons, with the majority of the mass between C4 and C10.

Geology: science that deals with the earth's physical structure and substance, its history, and the processes that act upon it.

Geophysical Testing: systematic collection of data for spatial studies; may use a variety of sensing instruments, and data may be collected from above or below the earth's surface or from aerial, orbital, or marine platforms; often used as part of the initial site exploration phase of a project.

Greenhouse Gases (GHG): gases such as methane and carbon dioxide which can accumulate in the atmosphere and cause the warming "greenhouse effect."

H

Half-Life: the amount of time required for a quantity of a substance to reduce to half its original amount. In the environmental context, it is the amount of time in which half of a compound or chemical can be expected to dissolve, evaporate, or decay into some other chemical.

Heating Oil: typically used in the operation of heating equipment, boilers, or furnaces; petroleum that is No. 1, No. 2, No. 4-light, No. 4-heavy, No. 5-light, No. 5-heavy, and No. 6 technical grades of fuel oil; other residual fuel oils (including Navy Special Fuel Oil and Bunker C); other fuels when used as substitutes for one of these fuel oils.

Henry's Law Coefficient (or Constant): the ratio of the vapor-phase concentration of an organic chemical relative to its dissolved-phase concentration in water.

Hydraulic Conductivity (of Soils): the ease with which pores of saturated soil permit water movement; a quantitative measure of a saturated soil's ability to transmit water when subjected to a hydraulic gradient (from http://nrcs.usda.gov).

Hydrogeology: combines knowledge of hydrology and geology to understand how water interacts with geological systems.

Hydrology: the study of surface and subsurface water occurrence, distribution, movement, and quality and its relationship with the environment within each phase of the water cycle.

I

ILO: Innocent Landowner.

Industrial Wastewater: produced as a byproduct of commercial activities; treated wastewater may be reused or released to a sanitary sewer or to surface water in the environment.

Inverse Condemnation: a cause of action against governmental entities for taking or destruction of a person's real property.

In-Situ: in its original place; unmoved; unexcavated; remaining in the subsurface.

L

Land Use Covenant (LUC): a recorded document which limits the current and future use of particular real property, both for the current owner and future owners.

Leachate: the liquid which is produced when groundwater percolates through **soluble** waste materials. "Leachate" or "leaching" can also refer to liquid chemical wastes migrating through underground soil and rock without the aid of groundwater.

Lead: naturally-occurring element found in the air, soil, water, and the earth's crust that is very toxic if it enters the body at high levels; commonly inhaled as dust, fumes, or mist which then enters the bloodstream and is stored in the bones.

Light Non-Aqueous Phase Liquid (LNAPL): "pure product" (i.e., gasoline) that remains undiluted as the original bulk liquid in the subsurface. LNAPLS (such as gasoline, diesel, other fuels, most crude oils, and creosote) are less dense than water; when petroleum is released into the environment, it is typically as a LNAPL.

Limited Phase II Environmental Site Assessment: sampling to confirm the presence of a pollutant.

Lower Explosive Limit (LEL): below the explosive/flammable range; mixture is too lean to burn; also known as "Lower Flammable Limit."

M

Maximum Contaminant Levels (MCLs): highest concentration levels allowed by law in public water supplies promulgated by the EPA and/or the applicable State environmental regulatory agency.

Methanogenesis/Methanogenic: fermentation by micro-organisms of simple organic carbon compounds or oxidation of hydrogen under anaerobic conditions with the production of carbon dioxide.

Method Detection Limit: takes into account the reagents, sample matrix, and preparation steps applied to a sample in specific analytical methods.

Micro-organisms: bacteria, fungi, protozoa, and actinomycetes typically found in soil that assist in the processes of biodegradation and/or natural attenuation and methane; methanogenic conditions prevail in many contamination plumes after all other electron acceptors have been used up by other members of the subsurface microbial community (from http://toxics.usgs.gov).

Mold: spores form when humidity levels exceed 40%; some species may cause fungal hypersensitivity, upper and lower respiratory issues, asthma, pneumonia, and other symptoms that are commonly associated with allergies, asthma, and the common cold.

Monitoring Well: a well constructed exclusively to monitor and/or sample conditions of a water-bearing aquifer, e.g., water pressure, depth, movement, temperature, or quality; provides controlled access for groundwater quality samples and hydrogeologic information.

Motor Fuel: petroleum or petroleum-based substance that is motor gasoline, aviation gasoline, No. 1 or No. 2 diesel fuel, or any grade of gasohol, and is typically used in the operation of an internal combustion engine.

MTBE: methyl tertiary-butyl ether, a gasoline additive introduced in 1979.

N

NAPL: Non-Aqueous Phase Liquid, a liquid which does not dissolve in or easily mix with water. **Gasoline** and **diesel fuel** are NAPLs.

National Pollutant Discharge Elimination System (NPDES): the National system for the issuance of permits under section 402 of the Federal Clean Water Act including a state or interstate program which has been approved in whole or in part by the EPA.

Natural Attenuation: includes a variety of physical, chemical, or biological processes that act without human intervention to reduce the mass, toxicity, mobility, volume, and/or concentration of contaminants in soil or groundwater.

NCP: National Contingency Plan.

Non-Detectable Concentrations: chemicals that are not detected in a sample above a certain limit, usually the quantitation limit for the chemical in the sample. Often denoted with the notation "ND."

O

Occupational Safety and Health Administration: (OSHA) purpose is to "assure safe and healthful working conditions for working men and women by setting and enforcing standards and by providing training, outreach, education and assistance"; signed into law by President Nixon on December 29, 1970 (via osha.gov).

OEHHA: The Office of Environmental Health Hazard Assessment, an office within California's **DTSC.**

Outsourcing: allows a business to hire a consultant/third party only when needed in order to focus on managing the operations that are vital to their success.

Overall: a release that occurs when a tank is filled beyond its capacity.

Over-excavation: additional excavation needed after an underground storage tank and the surrounding soil have been removed; confirmation samples are collected from the walls and floor of the excavation pit and sent for laboratory analysis to ensure that the remaining soil does not present a threat to groundwater.

Oxygenate: fuel additives (alcohols and ethers) that contain oxygen, which can boost gasoline's octane quality, enhance combustion, and reduce exhaust emissions.

P

PCBs: polychlorinated biphenyls. This is a group of synthetic organic chemicals that can cause a number of harmful effects. PCBs were historically a major constituent of major hydraulic fluids (trade name: Aroclor) routinely used in hydraulic lifts. Both the **USEPA** and the International Agency for Research on Cancer (IARC) have determined that PCBs are probably carcinogenic in humans. There is no known natural source for PCBs in the environment.

PCE: an abbreviation of "perchloroethylene," another name for **tetrachloroethylene.**

PEA: Preliminary Endangerment Assessment. This is a procedure outlined by California's **DTSC,** whereby a **PRP** can determine "whether current or past waste management practices have resulted in the release or threatened release of hazardous substances which pose a threat to public health or the environment" as a prelude to potentially releasing the site from further action.

Perc: a shortened form of "perchloroethylene," also known as **tetrachloroethylene.**

Phase I Environmental Site Assessments (Phase I ESA): a safeguard which limits a property owner's exposure to environmental liability; goal is to determine the presence of any hazardous substances or petroleum products in, on, or at a property; includes records review, site reconnaissance, interviews, and report preparation.

Phase II Environmental Site Assessments (Phase II ESA): typically occur after a recognized environmental condition is discovered during a Phase I ESA; includes sampling and laboratory analyses to confirm the presence or absence of hazardous substances or petroleum products.

Photoionization Detector (PID): a portable vapor and gas detector that measures a variety of volatile organic compounds and toxic gases; uses ultraviolet light to break down VOCs in the air into positive and negative ions.

Physico-Chemical Properties: shorthand phrase referring to the physical and chemical properties of a given chemical or compound; properties are needed to evaluate fate and transport of chemical; including, but not limited to, aqueous solubility vapor pressure, density, Henry's Law Coefficient, specific gravity, and biodegradability.

Polycyclic Aromatic Hydrocarbons (PAHs): chemical compounds that consist of fused aromatic rings. Some of these compounds have high toxicity values and have been identified as carcinogenic, mutagenic, and/or teratogenic.

Polyvinyl Chloride (PVC): a polymer formed essentially of long chains of **vinyl chloride** molecules. Commonly used in pipes, particularly for irrigation.

POTW: Publicly Owned Treatment Works. A publicly-owned sewage treatment facility.

Practical Quantitation Limit (PQL): the lowest limit that can be reliably achieved within specified limits of precision and accuracy under routine laboratory conditions for a specified matrix; based on quantitation, precision and accuracy, normal operation of a laboratory, and the practical need in a compliance-monitoring program to have a su cient numbers of laboratories available to conduct the analyses.

PRP: Potentially Responsible Party.

R

Radon: radioactive gas commonly found in geologic regions that have prevalent granite or shale deposits; cannot be seen, smelled, or tasted; second-leading cause of lung cancer in the United States.

RCRA: The federal Resource Conservation and Recovery Act.

REA: Registered Environmental Assessor. The REA program no longer exists, and so clients should be wary of this designation.

Receptor: human or other living organism with the potential to be exposed to and adversely affected by contaminants because it is present at the source or along the contaminant migration pathway.

Recognized Environmental Condition (REC): the presence or likely presence of any hazardous substances or petroleum products in, on, or at a property.

Regulated Discharge: point or nonpoint source discharge subject to the permit or approval requirements of state and Federal regulations and any diffuse surface or groundwater discharge to surface waters which has the potential to cause an exceedance of the water quality standards.

Regulated Substance: an element, compound, mixture, solution, or substance that, when released into the environment, may present substantial danger to public health, welfare, or environment; includes any hazardous substance as defined by CERCLA, petroleum, and any other substance determined by the environmental regulating agency (via PADEP).

Regulatory Compliance: describes the goals that businesses must strive to achieve in their efforts to ensure they know and satisfy relevant laws, standards, and regulations.

Remedial Action Plan (RAP): detailed summary of the environment issues found on a property during a site characterization; outlines a plan of action that illustrates which methods will be used to achieve cleanup goals.

Remediation: to clean up, mitigate, correct, abate, minimize, eliminate, control, or prevent a release of a regulated substance into the environment to protect the present or future of public health, safety, welfare, or the environment, including preliminary actions to study or assess the release.

Reportable Release: a quantity or unknown quantity of regulated substance released to or posing an immediate threat to surface water, groundwater, bedrock, soil, or sediment; release reporting quantities and requirements are state- and material-specific.

Reporting Limit: lowest concentration at which a contaminant is reported.

Reservation of Rights: in the insurance context, a letter from the insurer to the insured reserving certain rights, such as the right to withdraw from defending a claim if it turns out there is no coverage, or the right to recover fees paid by the insurer if there is no coverage or potential for indemnity.

Resource Conservation and Recovery Act (RCRA): give the EPA the authority to control solid and hazardous waste through the generation, transportation, storage, and disposal process; addresses the increasing problems cause by municipal and industrial waste.

Risk Assessment: process to quantify the risk posed by exposure of a human or ecological receptor to regulated substances; includes baseline risk assessments, development of site-specific standards, and risk assessment of the remedial alternatives.

RWQCB: Regional Water Quality Control Board.

S

Saturated Zone: subsurface zone in which all the spaces in the rock or soil are filled with water; the water table is the top of the saturated zone in an unconfined aquifer.

Sediment: solid fragmental material that originates from weathering of rocks and is transported or deposited by air, water, or ice; accumulates by other other natural agents such as chemical precipitation from solution or secretion by organisms; forms in layers; includes sand, gravel, silt, mud, till, loess, and alluvium.

Sick Building Syndrome: occupants of a building experience acute health- or comfort-related issues that seem to be directly linked to the time spent in the building; symptoms cannot be attributed to allergies, asthma, or the common cold.

Smear Zone: area where free product has been transported through soils due to a fluctuating water table; a zone in soil that is either above or below the water table at any given time.

Snow Fans: compressed air and water spray out through several nozzles, and the airflow generated by the large fans blows the air/water mix into the air as a mist to achieve long hang time–which allows for freezing to occur; function well in moderate winds and broadcast snow over large areas.

Snowmaking Automation: allows ski resorts to take advantage of small snowmaking windows while reducing energy use, manual labor, and risk of injury.

Soil: unconsolidated materials above bedrock.

Solubility: relative capability of being dissolved.

Spill Prevention, Countermeasure, and Control Plan (SPCC Plan): establish operating procedures for the prevention of, preparedness for, and response to oil discharges at specific non-transportation-related facilities that may reach navigable U.S. waters and adjoining shorelines.

Stakeholders: all parties with a direct or indirect interest in the outcome of any activity.

Stormwater Runoff: generated from rain and snowmelt events that flow over land or impervious surfaces and does not soak into the ground; operator of these sources may be required to obtain a NPDES permit before they can discharge water.

Stratigraphy: a description of the rock or soil strata in the subsurface, particularly the sequence of layers subsurface and in the atmosphere, and of concern for underground storage tank remediation sites due to their mobility and toxicity.

Superfund Site: any land in the United States that has been contaminated by hazardous waste and identified by the EPA as a candidate for cleanup due to the risks to human health and/or the environment sustainable yield of a significant amount of water to a well or spring.

SVE: Soil Vapor Extraction. A method of removing **VOCs** from the unsaturated vadose zone, the area of soil just above the water table (i.e. the saturated zone, or **aquifer**), using vacuum pipes. Sometimes used with **air sparging.**

SWRCB: the State Water Resources Control Board, a California regulatory board.

T

TCA: tetrachloroethane, a solvent. Not to be confused with **tetrachloroethylene (perc)** or **trichloroethylene (TCE)**, which are distinct from tetrachloroethane.

TCLP: Toxicity Characteristic Leaching Procedure, a test developed by the **USEPA** to determine the leaching potential of waste under landfill conditions. A successor to the Extraction Procedure (EP) test.

Tetrachloroethylene: a common dry-cleaning fluid, also known as "perc."

Tetraethyl Lead (TEL): an anti-knocking agent formerly used in "leaded" gasoline.

Tolling Agreement: an agreement between two people to pause the running of the statute of limitations as to particular claims, or all claims.

Topography: detailed description or representation on a map of the natural and artificial features of an area.

Total Dissolved Solids (TDS): amount of inorganic materials such as minerals, salts, metals, cations, or anions dissolved in water.

Toxic Substances Control Act (TSCA): EPA regulates the introduction of new or existing chemicals under this act; EPA can require reporting, record-keeping and testing, and restriction relating to chemical substances and/or mixtures.

Trichloroethylene (TCE): a common metal solvent or cleaner, and a chemical breakdown product of tetrachloroethylene.

TRPH: Total Recoverable Petroleum Hydrocarbons, a measure of the amount of hydrocarbons in a sample (without differentiating between the types of hydrocarbons).

U

Underground Storage Tank (UST): a tank and any underground piping connected to the tank that has at least 10% of its combined volume underground.

Underground Storage Tank Indemnification Fund (USTIF): goal is to provide a cleaner state of Pennsylvania by administering a fiscally-responsible program to reimburse eligible participants for reasonable and necessary expenses incurred from releases into the environment.

Underground Utility Markouts: involves a color code and symbols to label public utility mains below the surface; mains may include lines for telecommunication, electricity distribution, natural gas, cable television, fiber optics, traffic lights, street lights, storm drains, water mains, and wastewater pipes.

Unsaturated Zone: area between the ground surface and the aquifer's water table within which the moisture content is less than the saturation and the pressure is less than atmospheric; soil pore spaces in this zone may contain air or other gases; also known as the "Vadose Zone."

Upper Explosive Limit (UEL): above the explosive/flammable range; the mixture is to rich to burn; also known as the "Upper Flammable Limit."

USEPA: The United States Environmental Protection Agency.

V

VI: Vapor Intrusion.

Vapor Pressure: equilibrium between gas and solid; force exerted by the gas or vapor released by a liquid or solid substance in a closed container; an indication of a liquid's evaporation rate.

Vinyl Chloride: a colorless gas and a component of **polyvinyl chloride (PVC).** Vinyl chloride is a known carcinogen and a hazardous substance under CERCLA.

Volatile Organic Compounds (VOCs): organic chemicals that are easily evaporated at normal room temperature; BTEX chemicals, benzene, ethylene, glycol, formaldehyde.

W

Water Quality Objectives (WQOs): narrative on numerical criteria designed to define appropriate levels of environmental quality and to control activities that can adversely affect aquatic systems.

Wet Bulb Temperature: relationship between temperature and humidity; the lowest temperature that can be reached by evaporating water into the air and will always be less than or equal to the air temperature.

INDEX